CH00945619

CAILEAN GALLAGHER was bor:
gow and attended Balliol 'the :
He joined the staff of Yes Sc
first to analyse the propagand
fore taking on a strategic role to persuade Labour members to vote Yes. In an effort to repair any damage done and return to the Labour fold, he organised the 2015 general election campaign for Labour MP Katy Clark, before decamping once again to England to plunge into the history of the poor political judgment of socialists and organise health workers for a small trade union.

RORY SCOTHORNE, born in 1992, was raised in various bits of Edinburgh which he euphemistically describes as 'leafy'. His fiery articles (and hair) have punctuated Scottish debate since he co-founded National Collective, the cultural Yes organisation, in 2012. Upon realising he had been part of creating a monster, he fled to join the more cantankerous fringes of the Scottish Labour left, but somehow still has Yes-voting friends and political allies. A graduate of the Universities of Edinburgh and Sussex, he has coordinated, disparaged and radicalised various left-wing organisations, most lately Momentum Edinburgh.

AMY WESTWELL was born in 1993 and grew up in Leith. A *sans-culotte* at heart, she pretends to be a historian and has attended Glasgow and St Andrews University in this guise. She mainly studies the history of political thought, particularly the history of hating the rich and their way of life. She has sold her labour to some 14 employers, but has been most productive working against them with Unite the Union. Harbouring a misguided belief in the communist potential of workers' education, she intends to continue to read history while persuading the people that it is not really there.

SCOTT HAMES writes about Scottish literature and politics.

Roch Winds

A Treacherous Guide to the State of Scotland

CAILEAN GALLAGHER
RORY SCOTHORNE
AMY WESTWELL

Luath Press Limited

EDINBURGH

www.luath.co.uk

First published 2016

ISBN: 978-1-910745-58-8

The authors' right to be identified as author of this book
under the Copyright, Designs and Patents Act 1988 has been asserted.

The paper used in this book is recyclable. It is made from
low chlorine pulps produced in a low energy, low
emission manner from renewable forests.

Printed and bound by Bell & Bain Ltd, Glasgow

Typeset in 11 point Sabon

Contents

Foreword

THIS SPIKY PROVOCATION comes from three of the most compelling voices to emerge during the Scottish referendum. Veterans of that fever-dream may recall their blog *Mair Nor a Roch Wind*, which dealt savage kicks to the ideological shins of the pro-independence left throughout 2013–14. At that time, the *MNRW* collective spoke from within the Yes congregation whose bad faith it seemed determined to expose, dismaying the faithful with stinging rebukes against Nordic utopians, crypto-patriotism and cuddly visions of socialism-without-tears. Badly out of sympathy with the post-No surge, they have now sharpened their critique into a general assault on the 'social nationalist' consensus.

The result is this joyfully scathing and insolent book, sections of which will be hated by every figure in Scottish politics and commentary I can bring to mind. Many of their comrades on the Labour left will recoil at the sight of a Fife Candide hailing the best of all possible unions to an appreciative crowd of headless torsos. We later catch a pitiless glimpse of a senior Better-Togetherist outside the Falkirk ASDA, 'half-slumped, half-smiling in placid resignation, surrounded by activists clinging to their campaign boards like driftwood from a shipwreck'. If Yes-minded readers grin at these passages, they will find most of the book a cold and sobering shower – the kind that usefully clears your head.

The style of diagnosis is purposefully destructive. 'Where constructive criticism offers a little tinkering here, a bit of reform there, leaving itself open to assimilation into the broader sweep of the existing order', the authors urge a fierce and 'mutinous' rejection of devolved common-sense. This negative ardour draws on a rich literary heritage, notably the self-delighted violence of Dostoyevsky's Underground Man ('whether it's a good thing or a bad thing, smashing something is occasionally very pleasant too'). Style and ideology aside, there is a clear sense of de-mob catharsis in their biting critique of the Yes campaign, in which all three were formally involved. As they cheerfully explain, the authors joined Yes Scotland for Machiavellian reasons ('amoral politics has immense potential for good'), attracted by the referendum's potential for instability and ideological unmasking.

How far was that potential realised, and what openings and closures were generated by 18 September? The authors have their own answer, aiming to disturb rather than decode the prevailing thought-world. If they can (to their credit) be difficult to locate within the general entrenchments of post-indyref Scotland – alignments deep and shallow at once – their rhetorical swagger has a clearer pedigree. Their vatic myth-busting and merry eviscerations strongly recall the prose of Tom Nairn, whose trajectory they seem to be experiencing in reverse – from some accommodation with Scottish nationalism to a more militant communism – at a pace accelerated by the energy of the referendum itself. Their withering account of Nairn's contribution to the 'Scottish Ideology' is worthy of the man himself, and there may be a sneaking tribute in the book's abiding motifs of decay, corruption and zombie-dom.

This is a book of (and against) its own moment, but we can better appreciate its caustic energies by recalling its precursors in Scottish polemicism. To invoke the

8

cliché, Hugh MacDiarmid saw his role in public life as 'the catfish that vitalises the other torpid denizens of the aquarium'. There was much catfishing in 2014, both MacDiarmid's style of hectic animation, and in the internet sense of emotional manipulation behind dubious or borrowed identities. This book aims to reveal both the excited thrashing and fond movement-building of 2014 in its goldfish aspect. Some will argue that the authors' programme harbours quite as many soggy illusions as social democracy, but this ruthless and often romantic work of negation has its sights on shattering rather than enlarging the aquarium. (To be sure, fish who attempt this must prepare for rough winds as yet unfelt.)

The young authors write like three baby sharks in a sea of guppies, an approach unlikely to gather a consensus of its own. I write as an advocate of their prose, rather than their programme, but it is easy to admire their hunger for un-containment.

Scott Hames

those best able to imitate the fox have succeeded best
Niccolò Machiavelli

Acknowledgements

WHEN THE THREE of us started working on this book in early 2014, we had very specific ambitions. We wished to sketch a pastiche of something we called the 'Scottish Ideology', and place it in the context of the accelerating Yes campaign. As the political situation fermented, the referendum was fought and lost, and each of us moved between different jobs and courses of study, this project became less clear, and strung out over two years. Our ambitions and ideas expanded and contracted, we read widely and divergently, but persisted in coming together to work through our arguments and find ways of presenting them. This piece of work is the result of extended discussions over theories and metaphors, angst over who had deleted what in collaborative documents, and a writing system that came to be known as 'a trawler and two seagulls'. We have been lucky to have each other to work with in the exceptionally non-communist political community of modern Scotland, and also to share an enthusiasm for anti-recruitment songs, crude communist imagery and *The Hunger Games*. Together we have developed a writing tone which, for all its attempted gravitas, belies our natural timidity and general fear of the world.

Our thought and work has been formed through engagement with radicals (some of whom doubtless will not wish to be described as such) in Scotland and beyond who have always been willing to debate with us and share their ideas. We would like to thank Áron Kecskés, Cat Boyd, Stephen Boyd, Iván Eusebio Aguirre Darancou, Tom Eyers, Leigh French, Matthew Gallagher, Ewan Gibbs, Scott Hames, Peter Hill, Pat Kane, Abby Kerfoot, Jon Lansman, Jenny Morrison, Dave Moxham, Stephen Noon, Maddie Wells and Ariel Wind. We have learned from Dick Gaughan the art of troublemaking.

We would particularly like to thank Pat Boase and MA McDiarmid for providing us with a perfect place to write together in the summer of 2015. We are extremely grateful for the suggestions, criticisms and advice offered by Jenny Morrison and Peter Hill who gave us perceptive and crucial feedback on our entire first draft. Grateful thanks are also due to Lotte, Gavin and the rest of the team at Luath Press, and to Nat, whose fox adorns the cover.

The quotes in the text from work by Hamish Henderson are reproduced with the kind permission of the Literary Estate of Hamish Henderson. Lines from 'The World Turned Upside Down' are reproduced here with the kind permission of Leon Rosselson.

This book could not have been published without the help and patience of Gerry Hassan, who, while no doubt suspecting some delusions of grandeur, had the generosity and patience to guide us through the book-producing process.

How Scotland Got Carried Away

Roch the wind in the clear day's dawin
Blaws the cloods heelster-gowdie ow'r the bay
But there's mair nor a roch wind blawin
Through the great glen o the warld the day.
Hamish Henderson, 'Freedom Come-All-Ye' (1960)

TWO SHORT GENERATIONS after Henderson imagined Scotland being swept up into an international revolt against British domination, a rough wind blew through Scotland with a force that nearly pulled the United Kingdom apart. The Independence campaign hurled the hopes and aspirations of tens of thousands of Scots into the air, and after two years of blowing and howling, it carried them away. Forty-five per cent of voters opted for Scottish independence, many of them convinced that Yes could usher in a society governed in the interests of the people rather than those of a corrupted Westminster elite, for the benefit not just of Scots but of those across the world inspired by democracy and a better society.

This is the story Yes voters tell about the referendum: the campaign was a progressive, anti-austerity, anti-poverty, anti-war movement that lifted a people out of quietude and into political action. Every instance of this tale's recounting is another act in the beatification of an ossified saint, whose apostles are still moulding her miracles into folklore. When you're on the losing side of history, romanticism is inevitable. Political disruptions leave traces buried under the rubble of new events, and it is impossible to excavate them impartially. Over three and a half million people voted in the Scottish independence referendum, 84.5 per cent of the electorate. This was a record for any election held in the UK since the introduction of universal suffrage in 1918. Tens of thousands of activists were on the streets on 18 September 2014. These numbers are in the records, they are fossilised, like so much of Scotland's political and economic energy. The enchanting thing about fossils, especially for politicians, is that they are nought but traces. The little we can say about them is mostly supplemented by the imagination.

The independence movement has an uneasy relationship with its own past, be that the last five years or the last 50, but when a performance is required the people and events buried in the cemetery of history are made to dance. Our aim is not to join this *danse macabre*, but to dig up the remains, see what we make of the traces, and display the corpses in all their grisly glory. In this activity we are in good company, for while we are told that Scotland has a proud history of communitarianism, internationalism and socialism, it also has a history of grave robbers and resurrectionists: those who bring back into the light things that most thought better left buried.

So welcome to our gory bed, in which we make sense of what we find only by calling on the service of a broad cast of spirits of the past. The three of us have different views on political and economic domination and how to challenge it, but we are all indebted to, and break from, a Marxist tradition in a number of ways and in different directions. Our radicalism is rooted in the work of Gerrard Winstanley, Jean-Jacques Rousseau, Thomas Paine, Vladimir Lenin, Rosa Luxemburg, Simone de Beauvoir, Walter Benjamin, Theodor Adorno, Hamish Henderson, Hugh MacDiarmid, Edward Palmer Thompson, Raymond Williams, Dick Gaughan, Phil Ochs, Judith Butler, Leon Rosselson, Michael Marra – we could go on. No single doctrine underpins our thought; what holds us together is our commitment to radical freedom, and challenging capital by harnessing roch winds.

Stop the world, Scotland wants to get off

The Scottish predicament today calls for the same ruthless and objective appraisal which a general demands from his staff before action. Any attempt to fob us off with pious platitudes must be met with uncompromising hostility. The Scots had better realise that spiritual up-lift is no substitute for earthly élan. Hamish Henderson, on the Campaign for a Scottish National Assembly (1947)

THE YES AND NO campaigns described polarised futures. In one post-independence world, the pervasive political-economic doctrine of austerity would be overcome by a small nation on the fringes of Europe, and the energies of an unleashed Scottish economy would underpin a fairer distribution of new-found wealth. We, *the people of Scotland*, could then do things ourselves, reap our own harvest, ring our own till. Yes strategists tuned into the warnings about a failing welfare state that campaigners across the UK had been broadcasting since the crash. The SNP advised the people sagely to leave the misery of global economic tumult behind, via a trip to the polling booth. *Stop the world, Scotland wants to get off.*

In a parallel post-independence world, Scotland would be plunged over the brink of disaster, its dreams of a fairer, more prosperous future exposed as nothing but economic delusion and geopolitical naivety. To deny the compulsion of austerity was to deny the salience of massive economic forces that were sweeping the world. Quite clearly, an independent Scotland would not make a seamless transition to prosperity, but would be at the mercy of those far more powerful forces that had mandated the cuts to social protection, economic investment and public services across Europe. These forces, this climate, is 21st century capitalism, and the reckless advocates of Yes were asking Scottish people to believe they could confront it solo.

We didn't see it either way. The main platform for our interventions in the debate was the blog *Mair Nor a Roch Wind*, the title invoking a poem that noticed rough winds rushing through the world and called for a series of national revolts against the international order. It summed up the hopes – and the concerns – that we had during the struggle for independence. Perhaps in an independent Scotland, left politics could have become something much more than the elemental upsurge of hopes and ideas that gripped the country during 2014, and make some small contribution to breaking the control of the post-crisis ruling class in Europe and beyond. At least a Yes vote would have introduced some instability that would have threatened the comfort of Scotland's establishment – although it would also have encouraged them to consolidate their power.

In any case, Scotland voted No. But this event could not bring down the other-worldly dreams of thousands who had been carried away by the independence movement. The SNP was the primary beneficiary of the fervour that continued after the referendum. Its rallies were attended by thousands, such as the one in the Glasgow Hydro Arena on 21 November 2015 during which the various personae of the SNP appeared as strong as ever. And despite the resignation of the party's once-great chieftain, Alex Salmond, new heads kept growing: from new leaders, Nicola Sturgeon and Stuart Hosie, to young left-wing politicians like Mhairi Black, to former Tories like Tasmina Ahmed-Sheik and small-business owners like Michelle Thomson.

Sceptics recoiled as they watched the SNP take an almost mythological form: the Hydra in the Hydro. The power of a national populist party is to appeal to different identities and interests, and speak to all parts of society at once with the message of national prosperity. To assail it is a Herculean task, for which the party's most prominent opponents seem totally unprepared. Such a task involves sizing up the organisations and politicians that run the country and exposing them to the weapon of criticism, getting as close as possible to strike at their fleshy underbelly.

It is apparent to us, as we hope it will become to our readers, that the colossal shadow cast by the SNP obscures the real nature of Scotland and its politics. Whether this half-darkness comes before a dawn or heralds the start of a long night is still to be seen. But bands of the righteous still carry the torch of independence, seeking out another referendum – a way back to a lost way out. They insist, with MacDiarmid, that they are but Scots wha blin'ly follow auld Scottish instincts, never doubting that a giant monster lurks in the loch:

> Content to glimpse its loops I dinna ettle
> To land the sea serpent's sel wi ony gaff.[1]

We grubbier brigands assail this behemoth with a heavy heart, pessimistic about the fictional creature they find so inspiring. To hunt the serpent seems as misguided as the activity of those who scope out the depths of Loch Ness for a monster and find only tyres and rubbish. Naturally we expect that's all we will find – but still we confront the notion there is something else, some strange leviathan which keeps the Scots in awe. 'The old world is dying away, and the new world struggles to come forth: now is the time of monsters', said Gramsci, as he dismissed the unfounded optimism of those who believe in fictional futures. Fantasists, he said, are convinced that:

> One can do whatever one wants, and one wants a whole series of things which at present one lacks. It is basically the present turned on its head which is projected into the future. Everything expressed is unleashed. On the contrary it is necessary to direct one's attention violently towards the present as it is, if one

---

1 Hugh MacDiarmid, *A Drunk Man Looks at the Thistle* (1926)

wishes to transform it. *Pessimism of the intellect, optimism of the will.*[2]

In this book we do not presume to offer any penetrating new theoretical insights. But we do attempt to give an answer to the fundamental political question 'who, whom?' – who has power to do what to whom? What authority represents the emerging Scottish state, and what is it capable of doing (or not doing) to the people? Who is the creator of this new persona, and who is served by its stately deeds? Those in politics who talk across these questions with elevated fantasies for a future nation are never to be trusted.

So it is time to slay the Scottish Ideology for the greater good. It is our conviction that the Scottish politics of consensus sustains the exploitation of those who depend on selling their labour for a living, and any politician who claims to be acting in the interests of the working class but does not engage in behaviour that conflicts with capital's interests is either lying about their intentions or misinformed about the structure of society. Any reforms that are gained through agreement and consensus between the wage- and welfare-bound majority, and the administrators and representatives of the business world do little or no harm to the interests of the latter.

Classified

Implicit in this critique is our appeal to an alternative politics of class struggle. We retain this tired phrase because it is still the clearest term to discuss the way that

---

2   Antonio Gramsci, *Selections from the Prison Notebooks* (1929–35)

one class, held in common subjection and exploited in the name of profit, struggles to become unbound from this relationship. By invoking the working class we don't delineate a 'real' working class from those who are unemployed, disabled, retired and so on. Increasingly, different sections of the working class depend on selling their labour in irregular ways. Thus the way we think about the unemployed is increasingly similar to the way we think about those in short-term, insecure or part-time work. Many people slip constantly between conditions of unemployment and underemployment. The situation of underemployment has been encouraged in Britain to create a constantly available body of labour to be utilised and cast aside as necessary. One reason to be cautious about the term working class is that it invokes good old days of mass industrial labour in secure work, when men, and sometimes women, were able to use the power of collective organising to make demands on capital. This kind of working class is swiftly evaporating. The term's privileging of a specific kind of labour, normally productive manufacturing, creates blind spots. Women's unpaid work is denied class status. Life-long professional and public workers are exhausted before pensionable age. Hence our use of the term is deliberately broad, referencing all those who have a relationship of subjection within an economy driven by public or private capital which controls their work or their attempts to work.

Through our attempt to chart the condition of Scotland, we also intervene in strategic debates between socialists whose organisations have been torn between a range of different approaches to the referendum and to Scottish nationalism more generally. At risk of crass classification, their strategies can be roughly categorised under three slogans.

'Britain is for the rich, Scotland can be ours'

This was the mantra of the Radical Independence Campaign, for whom the Yes campaign was fundamentally about the interests of the Scottish working class. This part of the left rejected the Labour Party entirely. While it included many trade unionists it won little formal trade union support. Its relationship with the SNP was often ambiguous, sometimes critical, and occasionally explicitly supportive. It was a coalition of Eurocommunists, social democrats, Greens and former Trotskyists, instigated and directed by the International Socialist Group, a Scottish split from the Socialist Workers' Party. This group was united around the belief that an independent Scotland would provide firmer terrain for left-wing politics than Britain, thanks to its more progressive political discourse, its proportional electoral system, its lack of a strong Conservative Party, its capacity to break up an unreformable British state, and so on.

'Keep the red flag flying here'

At the opposite pole from the pro-independence left were the partisans of the Labour left, offering at their best a strange and bitter brew of old-guard Trotskyism and *Chavista* Stalinism. This part of the left firmly opposed independence on the grounds that it would divide a hitherto united British working class and remove the Scottish working class's capacity to challenge capital based in London, while providing business with an opportunity to instigate a race to the bottom in terms of wages and working conditions. In this view, the independence movement was always subordinate to the SNP, and enthusiasts of the pro-independence left were either the willing or unwilling lackeys of an embryonic Scottish national ruling class.

'Nationalism works for the rich, but so does everything'

A third, small and largely ignored fraction of the anarchist and grassroots activist left engaged enthusiastically with the referendum debate and offered some of the best critical analysis of both unionism and nationalism. Scottish anarchists in particular took a largely instrumental approach to the question of independence, either coming to support it as a means of building structures of resistance outside parliamentary politics, or opposing it based on a belief that things would not be any better with independence than without it. Whatever side they backed, these radicals retained a scepticism towards the promises of social democrats and socialists regarding the progressive potential of nation-led reform, be it Scottish or British. Many anarchists who supported independence have expressed disillusionment with the Yes movement since 2014.

Each of these positions is in its own way revolutionary. This book tries to take all of them seriously and to some extent on their own terms, moving beyond the kneejerk criticisms levelled by each against the other. As for ourselves, we are perhaps closest to the final category. We supported independence, but oppose nationalism and consensus politics. We suggested that radicals should prepare to engage with politics during moments that have a popular character, such as the referendum, because such events have a profound (and often irreversible) effect on political consciousness. At the same time, being pessimistic, we believed that radical potential in Scotland following the referendum was tiny. Given the global wealth divide and the ecological crisis coming in the wake of capitalism's untrammelled force, Scotland, a small national periphery of a former imperial power, seemed to be infertile ground for large-scale socialism. Determination to understand these limits, and readiness to pounce on whatever slight opportunities do arise, are the basis for a political strategy we call 'organised pessimism'.

According to this strategy, building strength on the basis of movements or parties is not enough. It is not only strength but also cunning that the left needs: not only force but also fraud. Cicero, the great conservative politician of the Roman Republic, was terrified of both because of their potential to disrupt the system of property, law, justice and offices that helped his aristocratic friends preserve their power. Concluding his discussion of justice, he warned that:

> While wrong may be done, then, in either of two ways, that is, by force or by fraud, both are bestial: fraud seems to belong to the cunning fox, force to the lion; both are wholly unworthy of man, but fraud is the more contemptible.[3]

---

3   Marcus Tullius Cicero, *On Duties* (44BC)

Yet Machiavelli, the great strategist of Renaissance Florence, urged that a political agent who seeks to up-turn justice and instate themselves must adopt bestial tactics. They ought to emulate both the fox and the lion, using both force and fraud,

> because the lion cannot defend himself against snares and the fox cannot defend himself against wolves. Therefore, it is necessary to be a fox to discover traps and a lion to terrify the wolves. Those who rely simply on the lion do not understand what they are about.[4]

This is the Machiavellian basis for our politics: to view all events, from the closure of a road-bridge to the crisis of the financial system, as an opportunity not only to threaten the government by force, but also to outfox the clumsy consensual politics that cover the cracks in society, challenge the legitimacy of law and order, and use treachery to unseat those in public office.

Dissecting the body politic

Of the series of famous anatomists working in Edinburgh in the early 19th century, Dr Robert Knox was the most renowned. Knox's penetrating insights brought to light more than the others. The reason? His corpses were the freshest of all – acquired at first by grave-robbing, but soon afterwards by a far more sinister practice. In Edinburgh, over about ten months in 1828, William Burke and William Hare committed 16 murders and sold the corpses to Dr Knox. In his play on

---

4   Niccolò Machiavelli, *The Prince* (1513)

the subject, Dylan Thomas put Knox in no two minds:

> Observe precisely. Record exactly. Neglect nothing.
> Fear no foe. Never swerve from your purpose. Pay no
> heed to Safety.
> For I believe that all men can be happy and that the
> good life can be led upon this earth.
> I believe that all men must work towards that end.
> And I believe that that end justifies any means... Let
> no scruples stand in the way of the progress of medical
> science!'[5]

This book is an examination of the corpses unearthed since the referendum. Those squeamish about dissecting the rotten state of Scotland will hopefully find it uneasy reading. Our purpose is to present the remains for others to dissect.

The first cadaver we found when no-one was looking for it: the corpse of devolution. The folk ballad 'Twa Corbies' is about a knight who had not been seen for some time, abandoned by his hound, his raven, and his lady. He lies 'ahint yon auld fail dyke' having his eyes pecked out by two black crows, and the wind blows away his skin leaving nought but the bones. It is in this state that we find devolution, the great hope of the 1990s, now little more than a set of bones being pecked at behind the bins. This knight was never truly esteemed by the Scottish people, but was commissioned when an elite network, often known as Civic Scotland, put aside their feuding differences to fund its expedition.

5   Dylan Thomas, *The Doctor and the Devils* (1966)

The second corpse is more dated: the remains of the social democracy that thrived in Britain for the last few decades. If the history of 21st century Scotland started with devolution, this creature is prehistoric. It never evolved to survive the modern conditions of global crisis. Labour's cumbersome frame of mind dominated Scotland until a meteor crashed into the global economy bringing recession and the collapse of social democracy across Europe. It appears that social democracy has no future in Scotland, Britain, Scandinavia, or indeed anywhere in the world. This is not surprising, for the conditions for social democratic life were specific to an epoch of capitalism which is now in its death throes.

There is a sense however in which Scotland is a crucial exception to the almost universal destruction of social democracy. This is the subject of Chapter Three, which examines the peculiarly Scottish breeds of modern political economy. Even for the most unscrupulous anatomist, bodies under examination are meant to be dead first. But for John Hunter, distinguished Professor of Glasgow University, the body of Charles Byrne, the 'Irish Giant', was an object of so much desire that he employed a henchman to move in across the street from the unfortunate Byrne and follow him around. The spy reported on Byrne's health and condition, and watched carefully lest Byrne died and be buried at sea beyond the reach of Hunter. We find ourselves in a similar position regarding the Scottish Ideology, as we have come affectionately to call it. As we follow it around, hurling insults and taking notes, a mob of its ardent fans protest in Pythonesque tones that 'it's not dead yet'. They miss the point. It is not Scottish social democracy's death but rather its undeath that interests us. It is bizarre that such a slow and weary creature continues to enliven the Scottish political sphere.

But its time will come. If the SNP is Scotland's captain, determined to make Scotland an ark of placid governability amidst the choppy seas of crisis, then we look for and develop those things which make Scotland ungovernable: the party or parties of disorder. A more radical current of communism is warming up, in the form of popular, organised mutiny. Our criticism is not constructive but destructive – and that, if anything, is our 'programme', or our 'alternative'. If solutions and reforms are to be proposed, they should be proposed in order to break things apart, not to restore or resurrect them. Our focus is profane: the first step in overcoming Scotland's problem is to acknowledge that we have one. In our preoccupation with national renewal, we risk forgetting how to make trouble for those that have the cheek to try and govern us. In criticising Scotland and its new establishment in a destructive rather than constructive fashion, we hope to offer something that cannot possibly be absorbed into a unified, national project that seeks the consent and support of all it touches. What we hope to prove is that there can be no truly 'inclusive' nationalism so long as there are people with the pessimism – and perhaps also the hope – to insist on something better.

There is a moral drive which stifles radical action and reacts against the impulse to come into conflict with the powers that be. This impulse is one of the most compelling motives in soft-left politics: it is what generated so much involvement in the Yes campaign. But it is not politically effective. The basic lesson of political realism is that right is not mighty. A moral politics is impotent; amoral politics has immense potential for good. Our world, postmodern and postmoral, has left morality behind, and seeks the instrumentalism that we believe left-wing politics needs to embrace not with regret but with hunger. We promote the kind of Machiavellian instinct to set out towards ends of power and to use various political means that are not consistent with a *personal* morality or ethics of harmony and consensus. And we suggest a Machiavellian willingness to take events and manipulate fortune, rather than adhere to the code of chivalry that wishes for objectives to be gradually built through the consent and commitments of groups of good citizens. If socialism follows the moral instincts of the people it might as well become a church – with the convoluted and hierarchical form that creates so many paradoxes in religion. We push against the moral vein running through the communitarian paternalism of devolution, the Panglossian optimism of Labour, and the consensualism of the SNP. Rather than be swept up in the return to a crude religiosity, we in Scotland have a chance to try out something different: a reformation of radical politics that is setting out to bring about the end of the order itself.

And what is to take its place? A country that rediscovers its socialist imperative, restoring the demand to change its material constitution and class constitution. We bemoan the criminal waste of people's lives at the hands of bad bosses, the poverty of estates, the dependence on foreign exploitation, the complicity in war, the corruption of finance, the hangover of imperialism, the conceit of privilege, the self-satisfaction about welcoming but a handful of refugees. We bemoan but do not negate. Bad bosses only die with the end of capitalism, poverty lasts as long as private ownership of land, and there will be refugees as long as there are borders. Total negation cannot get far in Scotland, for civic nationalism lacks the power or the will. The Scottish Ideology thrives on these contradictions but offers no solution. Its model of economics is useless; it is blind to reality and has uninspiring ends, allowing no conflict and no route to freedom.

At Hame wi freedom

Popular movements for freedom were the concern of a set of Marxist historians writing in the middle of the 20th century, including EP Thompson, who studied the origins of working class organising and political strategy. Thompson's writing influenced Hamish Henderson, who worked to support folk culture using what he described as the 'idiom of the people'. But sometimes Henderson got carried away. He began to second-guess the nature of the highland stories and songs he was collecting, saying that 'the words that I have looked for, and must go on looking for, are words of whole love.'[6] Thompson retorted that with these words Henderson had 'sabotaged' the meaning of his work, shifting attention from people and their actions to the poet and the poem. He wrote to Henderson:

---

6   Hamish Henderson, *Elegies for the Dead in Cyrenaica* (1948)

> Remember always who you are writing for: the people of Glasgow, of Halifax, of Dublin... I don't mean always today, or for all of them – but for the vanguard of the people, the most thoughtful ones. You will know Mayakovski's reflections on the difficulty of writing 'big poetry – poetry genuinely created' which can be understood by the people... [You], more than any other poet I know, are an instrument through which thousands of others can become articulate.[7]

The language of the Scottish working class was never expressed or defined during the referendum. We – radicals – failed to combine the language of freedom with the everyday. We failed to make people at home with freedom, or to use their own language rather than relying on the rhetoric of politicians. This book is written out of recognition of this failure. Just as Henderson strayed from the path that more clear-headed theorists of popular culture were able to see through their historical study and working class organising, we feel radical activity during the referendum failed to empower people with the means to express the desire for freedom from capitalism. This book is a product of failures, and of our determination to keep trying.

The criticism of other radicals may seem unfair, but be assured we level at least as much criticism at ourselves. We all fell short in theoretical ability and practical activity – we were all unprepared for the referendum. While many of the ideologists we criticised convinced themselves people became more free

---

7   EP Thompson, letter to Hamish Henderson (February 1949)

through quasi-democratic processes, we despaired that people failed to find a way out of the cave where shallow slogans echoed round the walls and the shadows of the struggle for power and wealth vanished in the artificial light of nationalism. We realise that this insight was not virtuous, for we failed to do anything with it that brought freedom to anyone.

There is a conceit and frustration amongst opponents to independence about the people's engagement in the campaign, expressed as a general denial that it had radical potential. Popular engagement was naïve but it was genuine. Just as people once tramped miles to hear a radical orator, in 2014 people spent their evenings travelling to hear the case for an independent Scotland. While many were just listeners, some developed their own self-taught political consciousness. But in the end, the popular radicalism that stirred in Scotland created no more than a roch wind.

> *Sae come aa ye at hame wi freedom*
> *Never heed whit the hoodies croak for doom*
> *In your hoose aa the bairns of Adam*
> *Will find breid, barley-bree and paintit room.*
> Hamish Henderson, 'Freedom Come-All-Ye' (1960)

CHAPTER ONE

Raising the Tartan Curtain

IN THE DREICH early hours of 19 September 2014, the three of us stepped onto the wet tarmac of Holyrood Road. Yes Scotland's referendum night party in the foyer of Edinburgh's Our Dynamic Earth had been dire. Everybody important was bunkered away in a private room underground and the expensive booze at the bar had been shut off at 1.00am in accordance with Scottish licensing laws. The early trickle of results had been so dispiriting that the room's sullen silence was broken only by a solitary, inebriated cry of 'We hate the Orkneys' when the islands' emphatic No vote was tallied up on the giant screen.

We left long before the key regions started coming in. Crossing the road outside in a daze, we were oblivious to the small silver car speeding towards us. Suddenly cottoning on to the imminent collision, two of us sped up and made it safely across, but the third slipped in the rain, tumbling to his knees in front of the advancing vehicle. His desperate, last-minute leap out of the way was all that separated him from an untimely and yet bizarrely totemic referendum-night departure.

Others crossing over that night were not so lucky. Without looking, and its triumph seemingly secure, the Scottish Labour Party strode nonchalantly from the pavement towards its familiar spot in the middle of the road only to be flattened by a nationalist bandwagon that went on to carry 56 Scottish National Party MPs down to Westminster.

Comrade Khrushchev goes to Disneyland

Is there something you haven't said, in all these pages?
Is there some secret room, and you don't want to show it?
Did an unlucky break befall the Lucky Poet?
Just what do you stand for, MacDiarmid? I'm still not certain.
I don' wanna step behin' dat tartan curtain...
Hamish Henderson, 'To Hugh MacDiarmid' (1945)

In an article for *The National*, the newly elected SNP MP George Kerevan compared his party's journey south to Keir Hardie's first experience in the House of Commons:

> As the first independent representative of the working classes, [Hardie] immediately drew criticism from the media and establishment of the day. His attire – a cloth cap and tweeds rather than a silk topper and morning coat – was denounced for being common and an affront to the dignity of the House.[8]

The SNP, Kerevan believed, were facing the same treatment. In his account, the SNP was the heir to Labour's

---

8   George Kerevan, 'Tories should watch out for the Frisky 56', *The National*, 25 May 2015

long-abandoned mission to be 'a perceived threat to the established order,' bringing dissent and peculiar foreign habits from the 'Celtic fringes' to the rotten metropole.

Kerevan was riffing on a key SNP message: just like in the days before instant communication and air travel, we in Scotland now wave our MPs off down to Westminster, trusting them to navigate the customs of the British elite, cope with the strange braying of MPs in the House of Commons, and extract from this muddle political results which are in the interests of everyone in Scotland.

Another SNP MP, Mhairi Black, was subjected to an infantilising interview while travelling to London to take up her seat, and demonstrated a political sensitivity that belied her 20 years of age. When asked 'Are you nervous?' she replied instantly 'I'm not the one who should be nervous, the people who are responsible for so much poverty... they're the ones that should be nervous.' The voiceover to the interview expressed astonishment that this Glasgow University student was visiting London 'for just the third time in her life', but Black appeared unfazed by the big city. Attacking a 'system that doesn't care', she responded to patronising questions with humour and cunning. The Prime Minister, she was informed, thought that parliament was 'like school'. Her response was rapier-sharp: 'it might feel like his school, but my school was a bit different.'[9]

When Khrushchev visited the United States in 1959, seeking peace and trade, he took delight in using every opportunity to portray how wasteful, shallow and unfair American life was compared to the noble daily

9   *Channel 4 News*, 11 May 2015

existence of the Soviet people. The cancellation of a particularly exciting day trip caused him no end of distress:

> We have come to this town where lives the cream of American art... But just now I was told that I could not go to Disneyland. I asked 'Why not? What is it? Do you have rocket-launching pads there?' I do not know. Just listen to what reason I was told: 'We,' which means the American authorities, 'cannot guarantee your security if you go there.' What is it? Is there an epidemic of cholera there or something? Or have gangsters taken over the place that can destroy me? Then what must I do? Commit suicide? ... For me, this situation is inconceivable. I cannot find words to explain this to my people.[10]

The farce had to be displayed to Khrushchev's 'people', for whom he was simply a modest emissary. The SNP MPs behave at Westminster like a Soviet leader in Washington. Mhairi Black was lauded for refusing to sit in the 'MPs only' area of the Westminster cafeteria, and the party's MPs were reprimanded during their first days in parliament for clapping, taking selfies at the dispatch box, and generally failing to properly defer to the old institution. This news was received in Scotland with delight, as proof that our political life is a continent away from theirs and all the better for it.

But beneath all this the mandate the SNP delegation carried to Westminster was uninspiring. Their minor

---

10 'Text of Khrushchev Debate With Skouras', *New York Times*, 20 September 1959

disruptions of parliamentary convention from brazen applause to selfies on the front-bench were the flairs of a bland diplomatic mission to secure 'more powers for Scotland'. Thanks to the Conservative majority the SNP obtained little real power at Westminster, but during rare interventions their manoeuvres were all made with a special end in mind: gaining leverage over constitutional reform. Having initially said they would not vote on the repeal of the fox hunting ban – the issue is devolved and lacks any implications for the Scottish budget via the Barnett formula – the last-minute decision to oppose it was reportedly a factor in the cancellation of the vote in the House of Commons. Party leader Nicola Sturgeon justified her U-turn as a tactic in the fight for 'more powers':

> Since the election, David Cameron's government has shown very little respect to the mandate that Scottish MPs have. On the Scotland bill, reasonable amendments backed by the overwhelming majority of Scottish MPs have been voted down. The English votes for English laws proposals brought forward go beyond any reasonable proposition and look to make Scottish MPs effectively second-class citizens in the House of Commons. So, I think if there's an opportunity – as there appears to be here – and on an issue where David Cameron appears to be out of touch with majority English opinion as well, to actually remind the government how slender their majority is [sic].[11]

---

11   Rowenna Mason and Libby Brooks, 'Sturgeon: SNP will keep foxhunting ban in revenge against Cameron', *The Guardian*, 14 July 2015

The SNP treats Westminster as an alien planet where the elite lives and rules. They play to the sense, held throughout Britain, that there is a deep disconnect between the Westminster parties and the people they claim to represent, and that British politics has no organic relationship with everyday life. They diagnose a systemic problem. The 'system' described by Black 'doesn't care'. This means that there is no point making power at Westminster an ultimate goal, since even the most noble party operating in that state apparatus would probably end up going to war in the Middle East by mistake, or tripping up in the treasury and spilling coffee all over the disability benefits budget. The SNP MPs leave their nation-building at the border and replace it with a sneering dismissal of Westminster as an irretrievably corrupted mechanism of state.

The SNP never explain to voters *why* the problems with Westminster are so endemic. It could be something to do with the elite education system in Britain, the political makeup of key marginal seats, or perhaps the separation of powers between Crown, Lords and Commons. The SNP's silence on the issue allows all sorts of inchoate frustrations to align with their cause, and they offer a basic prescription: *Get rid of it! But until you can, leave the nasty business of Westminster politics to us, and we'll ensure it doesn't cause you any more trouble than it already does.* Westminster represents politics as people detest it. The SNP's caricature of British politics as irreversibly conflictual, detached, and hamstrung by particularistic haggling stands in stark contrast with their beloved Scottish model.

At Holyrood, politics is in fact little more than understated, consensual budget management in the 'national interest'. Since the establishment of the Scottish Parliament the block grant has been set by the Barnett formula that determines the Scottish budget relative to UK government spending. The cash is then divided between departments by the Scottish Government. Some departments absorb very little of the grant: these tend to be the ones whose ministers pass the time attending corporate, sectoral, civic and diplomatic functions, briefed to make statements about fair work, skills, training, culture, Europe and external affairs. Others, such as those concerned with health and local authorities, swallow up over three quarters of the budget. The Scottish Parliament has always had the formal ability to raise taxes, bestowed in the original devolution vote in 1997 when the people voted for the parliament to have 'tax-varying powers'. However, the Blair government only legislated to allow the Parliament to raise or lower the basic rate of income tax by up to three per cent. It is a function that successive governments have humbly declined to use (partly due to the cost of administering the tax changes). The culture of budget management in successive Scottish governments has been based on this devolution process of grant-and-spend rather than tax-and-spend.

Under a tax-and-spend model, governments and their electorates are acutely aware of how policies *re*distribute power and wealth between different groups. The rich never let them forget it. Under grant-and-spend, the grant-receiving government need not relate to its electorate in the same way. It does not have to deal with taxpayers' demands about how the budget is raised. The complicated politics of taxation occur at a distance, and need not be factored in by government or voters when considering spending decisions. Cuts can be explained away as a result of changes to the block grant made by Westminster, while investment decisions are met with relatively little scrutiny from taxpayers. This strangely suppressed fiscal atmosphere isn't entirely down to the structure of devolution. It is, at least partially, learned. The SNP suffered electorally when it tried to include a tax-raising policy as part of its 1999 'Penny for Scotland' election campaign, a policy intended to reverse the 1p income tax cut brought in by the New Labour UK government. Since then the SNP has trod more carefully on the terrain of tax policy.

Together with this function of budget management the Scottish Government has developed a model of consensus. The SNP has tried to govern in a manner that attracts the support, or at least the tolerance, of those public sector and third sector organisations, trade unions and business leaders, who have the potential to turn the public against the government on the issues that it most concerns itself with: the delivery and policy of devolved public services. In schemes like Community Jobs Scotland which funds third sector organisations to create job opportunities, the Living Wage Accreditation Scheme that gives companies accolades for paying a wage that covers the cost of living, and the Working Together Review which assembled employers, trade unions and academics to review Scotland's 'progressive workplace policies', the Scottish Government has brought together the institutional representatives of various conflicting social interests, positioning itself as the mediator that can stand benevolently above the fray. With long-winded consultation processes and committee sessions, every stakeholder is accommodated in a process of resolving social policy questions. Politics is confined to administrative and regulative tasks while the government builds and maintains the support of as many policy-minded people as possible. Even if government ministers cannot reach agreement they make a show of having sought it, with the implication that the outcome (their policy) must be just, for the input was fair. Any dissent is thus condemned as sectional and unconstructive. In handling the 'progressive' reforms of equal marriage, land ownership, rent controls and fracking, the ruling party has gone to great lengths to ensure that conservative interest groups – churches, landowners, landlords and the energy industry, respectively – are involved and appeased as much as possible within the consultation process. Proposals are duly moderated and the broadest possible consensus constructed around them, often to the disappointment of those who had forced the issues onto the agenda in the first place.

The SNP glorifies Scottish society's immunity from conflict, and wishes to broaden this frictionless sphere to include the currently reserved domains of the economy, foreign affairs, business and industry. When the Scottish state-keepers glare enviously at those economic and military powers wielded all too enthusiastically by the 'Westminster elite', they invite us to imagine themselves holding those same powers with all the care and delicacy owed to an object of distant, respectful desire. The economy and international relations, the

objects of fiscal and foreign policy, are precious but-
terflies; if fought over and handled roughly their wings
will be crushed, their antennae bent. The SNP apparat-
chiks arrive in Westminster as aspirant butterfly-keep-
ers, hoping to find the gentle insects a new home in the
lush greenhouse of Holyrood where they can be nur-
tured by a benign national caretaker class.

While George Osborne gives contracts and tax
breaks to his pals, the SNP aspires to manage the economy in order to provide work and wages for the people,
opportunities for small business, and skilled workers
for big business, in the interest of all. The SNP ideologues contrast their own bureaucratic political culture to the cronyism of Westminster, presenting their
aspirational political activity not as the government of
persons but the administration of things. Of course,
the principal reason Westminster politics contains so
much conflict, and the reason big business and the very
rich are so interested in UK departments and close to
UK ministers, is that fiscal, monetary and foreign policy powers determine the conditions of economic and
social order. Effective politics at these stakes is *bound*
to be confrontational: control of policy, taxation and
economic power has a profound impact on the con-
trollers of capital. Bemoaning Westminster's bullish
style is all very well, but the SNP seeks to throw the politics of clashing interests out alongside the form of the
UK Parliament where those clashes take place, having
conflated the two so strongly in the minds of the public. What they want is not only the end of elite par-
liaments and dirty deals, but also the end of politics
based on conflict and opposition. In creating a politics

of administration they hammer the last nail in the coffin of a certain socialist parliamentary tradition, which seeks to use the electoral strength of the working class to grant people real legal and political strength in their communities and workplaces. What distinguishes the SNP establishment from other governments is its apparent insulation from any crude manipulation by capital, and its immunity from the disillusionment and mistrust which afflict most western political systems today.

The purpose of all the SNP's posturing is to pull powers away from Westminster and shape a 'modern' Scottish state. With no desire to use the state to redistribute power or influence in the economy, the ministers merely seek to expand its distributive role, primarily in terms of providing social security, welfare and relief. They assume the poise of a social democratic party, ready to share power in the interests of the people in common – but they have no place for the conflictual parliamentary politics that transform extra-parliamentary conflict, in industry and society, into state-led redistribution. Rather, the SNP wants the idea of the state to wither away in people's minds, so that when people look to the activity of the future Scottish state, they see only a hastily drawn tartan curtain, behind which they assume complicated administration takes place. But even their highly bureaucratic Scottish Parliament feels the cold breath of capital on its back, and the SNP are gearing up for the process of using the powers of the state in all kinds of ways.

To understand how this conflict-free politics which dodges the eternal political battle between rulers and governed was created and sustained, and how it was used by the SNP so successfully, we need to tear our gaze away from the shimmering dust thrown up in the bandwagon's wake and look to its route along the high road: through the landscape of devolution, the rise of the SNP, and the collapse of Scottish Labour.

Casting the establishment

Most political systems develop over centuries: parties develop to represent interests or ideologies, align with social and economic groups, and vie for control of state power. But the Scottish Parliament was conceived in a lab, and delivered by a Labour Party reluctant to hand Scotland the sort of governing apparatus that might give those who control it the appearance or re-sponsibilities of a national government. Its command-ing heights were named *The Scottish Executive*. Its au-thority was devolved from Her Majesty's Government.

After much ado about the Parliament building itself, when any faith in budget management was undermined as the cost rose from the initial £40 million estimate to a final figure of over £400 million, the Members of the Scottish Parliament (MSPs) found themselves in a struc-ture designed electorally and architecturally to produce non-oppositional politics. In this play-pen parliament, politicians shuffle papers and snipe behind each other's backs about mismanagement and manipulation of the committee structures like Douglas Adams' Vogon bu-reaucrats. They read out turgid speeches in the round consensual space of the chamber, feeding lean politi-cal issues into the rhetorical grinder and churning out mince. Then they toddle off to their respective meetings to issue curt opinions and scroll through twitter, yawn, attend a drinks reception in the parliament lobby, and go home. Its processes may lack Westminster's archaic rituals, but it is certainly just as stale. If Tony Blair is right about anything, it's that the Scottish Parliament has all the democratic energy of a parish council.

Labour and the SNP each have their own mythic accounts of the creation of this system of governance and its contribution to bringing about a referendum on independence. The Scottish nationalists present devolution as part of a dance to the music of nationalism taking Scotland gradually towards independence. Labour present it as a beneficent response to the demand for popular power, guided and created by themselves, the party most in sync with people's experiences. The common ground between the two interpretations is populated by that strange entity called Civic Scotland, comprising of vaguely 'representative' organisations that supposedly harnessed popular devolutionary demands in the 1970s and 1980s. The nationalists were, at the time, suspicious of Civic Scotland and its links with the Labour Party, but in retrospect they portray it as the early institutionalisation of an expanding nationalist fraction of Scottish political culture. For Labour leader John Smith, Civic Scotland expressed a 'settled will of the Scottish people' that stopped at devolution. Civic Scotland became the main proponent of an emerging consensus that stifled Scottish politics between the 1980s and the coming of the referendum; it is often understatedly utilised but little discussed now, because it has become part of the furniture in the story of Scottish political development. This omission conceals all sorts of important peculiarities.

The crucial feature of both Labour and SNP accounts is a belief that from the 1970s to the 1990s Civic Scotland and the parties that listened to it were expressing popular sentiments and demands for a Scottish Parliament. To put it otherwise, the Scottish people were lucky to have such benevolent and responsive leaders. These leaders were drawn from the various institutions and interest groups of Scottish society: political parties, trade unions, business interests and religious groups, which eventually coalesced into the Scottish Constitutional Convention.

But this small, slow-moving and broadly consensual constellation of organisations and individuals had little actual basis in popular political engagement. Former Labour MP and independent MSP John McAllion has been one of the few voices with experience of the events to break ranks from the conventional account:

> The Scottish Constitutional Convention claimed at the time that it was open, inclusive, and broadly-based, but in fact it was none of those things. It was self-appointed, it was elitist, and it was ultimately unrepresentative.[12]

Devolution politics were the politics of an elite. The form taken by constitutional politics in the era precluded the involvement of working-class organisations because the traditional forms of working-class politics in Scotland – industrial, member-driven, conflictual, aiming for power, and serving the immense majority against elite interests – were ruled out by Civic Scot-

---

12   Quoted in Connor Beaton, 'Ex-MP: Scotland 'in trouble' if lax on constitution', *The Targe*, 8 December 2013

land's cross-class, cross-party and constitutionalist character. The involvement of the trade unions in the Constitutional Convention did not alter its basic nature. Despite the support of the Scottish Trade Union Congress (STUC) for autonomous working-class action during the miners' strike and the anti-poll tax campaign, its constitutional adventurism marked a scission between a class-oriented industrial politics and a classless engagement with the parliamentary sphere. In devolutionary folklore, the last gasp of the Scottish labour movement as an autonomous entity was in the proposition of a 'workers' parliament' by the STUC during the Upper Clyde Shipyard (UCS) work-in, when workers responded to the threat of closure by taking over the operation of the yard. This early flash of constitutional radicalism, somewhat overplayed by Scottish labour historians and never developed into any formal proposal, gradually faded into the politics of consensus as the STUC worked with the Constitutional Convention to create a constitutional solution that had no particular industrial or class-based priorities.

This separation of industrial politics from political engagement reflected a widespread refusal on the left during the 1970s and 1980s to come to terms with the labour movement's dissolution. The radical left, which spanned from the STUC and the trade unions to the established Communist Parties and the Scottish Campaign for Nuclear Disarmament, was searching desperately for a new theoretical model as Marxism-Leninism declined alongside its traditional organisations. Many seized upon the Eurocommunist alternative which was then sweeping Europe's communist establishment: broad coalitions seeking power through liberal democratic institutions were now preferred to the old revolutionary class antagonism. An intelligentsia positioning itself at the head of the working class struck out bravely towards a new movement politics, but forgot to invite the workers along for the ride. Meanwhile the integration of the labour movement's baronial leadership into Civic Scotland occurred in tandem with the disintegration of the organised working class. The assaults on the working class throughout the Thatcherite era left traditional institutional systems and resilient communities weak and defensive. Even the 'workers' parliament' was proposed during a rear-guard action. UCS was more useful as an international symbol of workers' ongoing struggle than as an assertion of labour movement control, and the workers' parliament served a similar theoretical function.

Similar histories could be told about other 'representative' groups involved in Civic Scotland. In the absence of a formal Scottish state from 1707 the expression and regulation of civil society was carried out by the Kirk, legal apparatus, and universities, institutions officially preserved by the Act of Union. When these were represented as part of Civic Scotland in the devolution era, they claimed to be institutional evidence of a Scottish nation. In doing so, they disguised or dissolved their particular concerns and fields of knowledge in their congenial involvement in a Scottish consensus.

The narrative became widespread in Scotland that the state's means of understanding the will of the people should be to consult the mediator between itself and the people, the institutions of civil society. These institutions are now less typically conservative than the terrible trio of church, education and law, and comprise the third sector as well as publicly funded and constituted bodies. Thus since its formation in 1999 the Scottish Parliament and Government have made extensive consultation exercises the central feature of policy-making, bringing interest groups and associations round the table to discuss Scotland's future. The details of policy and its enactment are often less significant than the consultation process itself. To give the process maximal publicity and legitimacy, the government affords sufficient time and funds for tight campaigns on each side led by professional consultants and strategists. The consultation culture gives interest groups such as the Scottish Women's Budget Group, Shelter Scotland or The Poverty Alliance a cosy place near the heart of government, and their contributions are published in a range of official documents, but no serious action is taken by the government, for instance on women's work and wages. The tendency of the Scottish Government to view all kinds of organisations which advocate for and service oppressed sections of society as somehow *representative* of those people, or even particularly expert in their experiences, further estranges the policy makers from the people.

In the case of same-sex marriage, a policy process which was instigated in Scotland before it began to be considered in England, whole movements were mobilised under the opposing banners of 'Equal Marriage' and 'Scotland for Marriage' to march and lobby for and against a policy the government was in any case supporting. The law that ended up being enacted after years of internal discussion was more trans-inclusive than the equivalent UK laws, but the public discussions focused on the large mainstream campaigns fronted by Labour careerists and Church traditionalists. The policy was decided upon and shuffled into the civil servants' in-tray, who took so long to implement it that England had already held its first same-sex marriage by the time the law was in force in Scotland.

Thus the apparatus of devolved Scotland has developed to appear inclusive and representative, without being the result of any authentically popular involvement. The government has the power to consult on only those issues it wants, almost as a company would vet the proposals that reach its board or a bad trade union would weed out contentious motions ahead of its conference. The process is now so embedded, and the SNP so used to being able to control these predictable processes, that they are caught off-guard when democratic organisations force an issue into the political fray. In an exception that proves the rule, the SNP's 2014 consultation on short assured tenancies spiralled out of control, as the Living Rent Campaign, a non-establishment campaign for rent controls, jumped on the process and tried to use it to its advantage. Flooding the first consultation in late 2014 with responses,[13] three quarters of respondents called for government action to halt soaring rents. Displeased with the result and the anger it drew from landlords, the government launched a second consultation in 2015, which like-

---

13   The Scottish Government, 'Consultation on a New Tenancy for the Private Rented Sector', October 2014

wise was flooded with 7,500 responses.[14] Only the tumult of the referendum made popular initiative intrude into the civic setup of devolution Scotland, raising divisive issues often for the first time. In the case of living rents, the idea of a community of compatible interests was exposed as a sham that ultimately suited the landlords; and the social pressures of living in the rented sector were traced to the economic interests of buy-for-let owners.

The cage for left-wing nationalism

You can really have no notion how delightful it will be
When they take us up and throw us, with the lobsters,
out to sea!
Lewis Carroll, *Alice in Wonderland* (1865)

The consensualist trajectory of Scottish politics may seem contradictory, since Civic Scotland and the Constitutional Convention were formed in the context of the struggle against the same Thatcherism that decimated countless working-class communities. The Scottish constitutional turn was motivated by an aloof moral distaste, felt by the middle classes, towards the disasters experienced by Scottish communities under Thatcher. But it was not a plausible political strategy for an emerging political elite to oppose the forces responsible for financialisation. When Alex Salmond claimed in 2008 that 'we didn't mind the economic side [of Thatcherism] so much, but we didn't like the

---

14   The Scottish Government, 'Second Consultation on a New Tenancy for the Private Sector', March 2015

social side at all,'[15] he expressed the communitarian moralism that has stifled and subsumed the Scottish working class response to Thatcher's desocialisation, her encouragement of small businesses, her sale of council housing, and her debasement of the economy from industry to services.

The assumption that the Scottish people could be boiled down to a set of moral sentiments imbued the devolutionists with the self-important belief that they understood and expressed a 'national interest'. This sense was simultaneously nationalist, in that it imagined a common interest across antagonistic social forces, and social democratic, in that it identified this interest with the defence of a welfarist social settlement. People with administrative and professional roles in the management of the welfare state felt their benevolent way of life was undermined by Thatcherism, and so they pushed for devolution, justifying this with a now-common myth of Scottish communitarianism. This was the moment when a social welfarist politics became sutured to a Scottish national spirit. These are the origins of what the SNP and their hangers-on call civic nationalism. Social nationalism is a better term.

The history of most nations' politics are histories of power and struggle, but Scotland's political history tells the tale of a bunch of trumped-up administrators and entrepreneurs. The politics of devolution was, and is, predominantly concerned with the people of Scotland chiefly insofar as they interact with public services. The Parliament is a huge social provider, and only

---

15 'Alex Salmond: Scotland "didn't mind" Thatcher economics', *The Scotsman*, 21 August 2008

a state insofar as it regulates a small part of the human material of the economy: training people, regulating their activities and meeting some of their basic needs. The driving principles amount to equal opportunity to access whatever goods the Scottish Government can provide, equivalent to devolving Blairism, or the idea that social change is created through interventions in people's non-economic lives. Insofar as economic intervention happens, it fuses the government's education strategy with the government-funded Scottish Enterprise. Wendy Alexander embarked most enthusiastically on these waters with her Smart, Successful Scotland project to bring education and 'lifelong learning' together with 'Enterprise Networks' to help businesses 'contribute to our shared aims, our vision, to create a smart, successful Scotland', combining education with enterprise in a model the SNP continue to use.[16]

The parties of the Scottish Parliament are therefore thoroughly *bourgeois* in an old pre-capitalist sense, primarily concerned with people as they operate outside the economy. They deal with citizens, not workers. Trained only in the tools of welfare economics, the consensus is that all a government can do for the working class is implement measures to improve people's ability to enter or remain in a labour market that lies outside the state's control or influence. Skilling-up individuals, attracting business to Scotland, preventing sick-leave by reducing ill-health, and creating 'shovel-ready' projects: the work of a glorified municipality, not an aspirant state.

16 The Scottish Executive, 'A Smart, Successful Scotland: Ambitions for the Enterprise Network', 2001

While the devolved Parliament is certainly important, and does some mildly progressive things and so on, it's also very *tedious*. The structures of devolution keep out the elements of politics that are the most important and relevant for the working class. The remit of Scottish politics in administering social services to the citizens of Scotland excludes the issues of most salience for gaining control over the economy. The underlying dynamic of political and economic change, the conflict between antagonistic social forces, is contained within an administrative framework which claims to mediate between these forces. Politics as conflict spanning the whole of the social order has never been introduced to devolved Scotland, where politics is limited to a narrow set of widely shared civic interests. Devolution is a lobster pot: the creatures of Scottish politics are trapped in the mesh of consensus, pincers snapping feebly in the face of powers far outside their reach. Lenin's dictum was that communists should only ever stand one step ahead of the people.[17] In Holyrood, politics and people are an ocean apart.

The half-born nature of the devolved system explains all sorts of peculiarities. Most importantly, Labour's decision to give Holyrood control of the issues on which its managerial right felt most comfortable, rather than those rooted in the best traditions of the labour movement, is at the root of its failure to capitalise on its status as founder. It was instead the SNP, whose ambitions for Holyrood greatly exceeded those of Labour, who were able to build on the paltry foundations put in place by Dewar and Blair.

When Labour were first getting acquainted with civic nationalism in the 1970s, the SNP's politics were separatist, cranky and oil-fired. Its leaders were torn between sustaining a moderate rural and small-town vote in the north-east and winning Labour voters in the central belt. Some members, on the lookout for ways to advance their cause, saw a new emerging reaction develop in response to Thatcher, in particular the mobilisation against the Poll Tax. They developed an electoral interest in the working class. A group of SNP members that came to be known as the "79 Group' sought to 'equip itself with a strategy for building an anti-Tory coalition of Scottish interests around a working-class core'.[18] They were expelled for the challenge they presented to nationalist orthodoxy by emphasising the politics of class. But in the words of leading '79er Stephen Maxwell, even they were 'more interested in... the SNP's electoral prospects than they were in confronting the dilemmas of modern socialism, or in constructing a credible socialist programme for Scotland'.[19] Questions of political economy and the distribution of power and wealth had a role to play in this particular ideological tributary of modern Scottish nationalism, but that role was ultimately instrumental rather than radical. When Maxwell asked 'whose Scotland?' in his essay 'The Case for Left-Wing Nationalism', he implied that the answer 'ours' could eventually come from the working class. But the SNP was bound

18 Stephen Maxwell, *The Case for Left Wing Nationalism* (2013)

19 Maxwell, *Left Wing Nationalism*

to answer first, for any consideration of class interest was subordinated to national interest.

It was this increasingly pragmatic and instrumental approach to ideological positioning that allowed the SNP to practice social nationalism better than the other parties. Salmond, a member of the '79 group himself, gradually abandoned the emphasis on civil disobedience and class politics that had resulted in his expulsion from the party. As the political usefulness of the working class waned under the attacks of the 1980s, Salmond's sympathies flitted from labour to capital with ease. In the 1990s he spoke to the interests of Scottish businesses damaged by a monetary policy which privileged South East England. This was still couched in a liberal and nationalist moralism. Salmond is known to insist that Adam Smith's *Wealth of Nations* be read alongside his *Theory of Moral Sentiments* in order that the moral philosophy underpinning a prosperous free economy is not undermined. For Salmond this moral system is, of course, Scottish society, with its communitarian Scottish values. Salmond's ascent to dominance of the SNP epitomised the party's drift towards this chameleonic approach to ideology. Anchored securely to the overriding goal of independence, the nationalist ship was allowed to drift to wherever the waves of Scottish public opinion took it.

In a system where class is already excluded, and all parties uphold a uniform politics because it is the way to win power, there are only a certain number of political tricks that need be performed in order to appear solid and reliable. The SNP's victory in 2007 was their reward for rebranding from a separatist to a Holyrood party, interested in using devolution in a way that Scottish Labour was unable to. Scottish Labour's subservience to the increasingly unpopular UK Labour Party made the limits of devolved Labour politics too obvious to bear. Jack McConnell is most culpable in this regard. When the Scottish Executive embarked on its first major public works effort, he energetically embraced Brown's Private Finance Initiative to fund new infrastructure. When the imprisonment of child refugees at Dungavel Detention Centre was being attacked on all fronts, he could not muster the courage to stand up to Blair. The SNP's political substance – public service universalism with a frisson of symbolic anti-war excitement – was as banal as their institutional basis, but they brought to this banality a style which both distinguished them from Westminster and made them seem like the right people to spice up a parliament which was already becoming stale in the eyes of its electors. 2007 was a victory built not on policy but on Salmond's swagger, a sharp media operation, and an earthy social nationalism which contrasted with the cosmopolitan cynicism of the Blair years. The SNP made the parish council seem like a proper parliament, where policies cohered in a single national purpose.

They aligned themselves with the requirements and structure of governing in Holyrood, successfully concealing the contradiction between gradualist means and nationalist ends. Their gradualist strategy worked: they developed an image as the natural party of stable and competent devolved governance, putting independence to one side as devolution took priority. But they were rewarded so overwhelmingly in 2011 by an electorate reduced to a mass of service-using Scots that their underlying *raison d'etre* came rushing to the surface. The possibilities afforded by majority rule took both the party and their voters by surprise.

Yes Swampland

The SNP was adept at speaking to Scottish interests, and trusted to administer rather than rule, winning a remarkable victory in 2011 on the basis of their 'Record, Team and Vision': a record of competent administration by a team of popular politicians, and a vision of a glimmering, green, reindustrialised homeland. The victory brought with it the unexpected independence referendum. Having become a party of devolved government, the SNP now had to develop a campaign for an independent Scotland, and connect with the sentiments of the people, a task for which their strategists and MSPs were completely unprepared. From the swamp of Holyrood, immersed in devolved governance but without an instinct for the economic and social experiences of those that it needed to win round, the SNP had to drag itself onto the people's level: to understand their fears and engage them in a movement.

It is easy to read back from the 2015 election result and suppose that the SNP had an instinct and connection with the people right from the start. In fact, the distance of their politics – and all devolved politics – from everyday economic experience was the root of their inability to engage with hard material concerns. Initially confident, the SNP realised that in order to win they needed a campaign that brought the people's problems back into politics.

Yes Scotland was the arm's-length campaign whose role was to create a Yes brand, foster local and sectoral groups, and present a non-SNP message to media and the public. From its launch in summer 2012 until spring 2013, Yes Scotland broadcast a vague sense of managerial optimism that spoke more to third sector mandarins than those living in areas of deprivation. Their strategy was premised on the idea that 'influencers' from each sector of society, convinced of the imbalance of power across the UK and persuaded that an independent Scotland would be fiscally sound, would relay the case to the people. It was as if the campaign could be fought in a bubble, as if winning the professional class responsible for the previous wave of constitutional politics was the surest route to popular backing. In the early days, the Yes Scotland economic line was that a Yes vote would help 'rebalance' the economy of the whole UK, providing opportunities for business and giving the Scottish Parliament levers to secure and direct investment that would improve life for everyone.

Throughout the campaign's early stages the message-makers in Yes Scotland had remained deep in the managerial swamp, sending up fat bubbles of optimism about 'fairness' and 'prosperity'. Their approach, which peaked with the White Paper, was to emphasise continuity over any significant material change. The SNP mindset was that people were only interested in another step along the devolution road. Their Draft Scottish Independence Bill, which sketched the constitutional transition process to independence, claimed that with independence, 'many of the structures and workings of the existing Scottish Government can continue and, with the added powers of independence, would extend to cover the policy areas currently reserved to Westminster'.[20]

When this strategy brought little joy, the generals in the SNP changed course. The Yes campaign took on a popular aspect, which clashed with the conservative appeal to continuity. The referendum coincided with cuts to benefits, wages and employment on an historic scale. The UK and international response to the financial crisis of 2008 was the major context, and ending austerity became an obvious and overriding argument for independence. So it was in June 2013, long after anti-austerity activists were calling for a Yes vote, that Yes Scotland finally started talking explicitly about halting a worsening situation, and taking a route out of the austerity of alternating Labour and Tory governments. No plan of any substance was offered as an alternative to austerity, beyond a totally insubstantial increase in public spending. But the message became a mainstay of the Yes campaign and later of the SNP's 2015 election campaign. As it developed this anti-austerity pitch, Yes Scotland began to 'resource' the grassroots organisations that had emerged independently, and over which the SNP had little control. In the early stages of the campaign, many of these had radical demands: Trade Unionists for Independence had a socialist programme of opposition to austerity that it intended to promote through trade union networks; Women for Independence included socialist feminists who demanded that independence for women must

---

20   The Scottish Government, 'The Scottish Independence Bill: A consultation on an interim constitution for Scotland', June 2014

extend to economic freedoms; and the Radical Independence Campaign injected the far-left's instinct for conflict into the burgeoning movement.

As these groups entered Yes Scotland's orbit, their power and autonomy diminished. Those who took their own path were sent spinning into the void: the ambitions of 'Trade Unionists for Independence' were seen by senior SNP figures as too divisive, so the group was sidelined and replaced by the in-house 'Trade Unionists for Yes'. Run by four trade unionists integrated with the SNP hierarchy, its core purpose was to present trade unionists as broadly in favour of the SNP's agenda for independence, and to set out the advantages of a Yes vote for trade union members: slightly higher wages, better union-business partnership, and a review of workplace rights. There was no attempt to strengthen the labour movement's hand ahead of a Yes vote.

National Collective, the cultural campaign for independence, was established by a set of young bohemians and intellectuals eager to stir some colour into the campaign's bland designs. Initially lukewarm towards the SNP and occasionally at loggerheads with Yes Scotland's cultural organisers, it was courted as it toned down an initially radical message such that by the time of the referendum its leaders were coordinating action with the SNP. Women for Independence was caught between a broad group of feminists determined to promote a new definition of 'independence for women' in Scotland, and SNP careerists who were anxious to dilute its feminism in order to promote the SNP's headline childcare offer and similar 'women-friendly' policies. Through integration into the official cam-

paign, the voices of these groups became more controlled, and the power of critics was curtailed by the
SNP's demand for fealty. The most interesting case was
the Radical Independence Campaign. Initially Yes
Scotland kept their distance from the politics of conflict
and aggravation that underpinned RIC's message. This
was, after all, a creation of the International Socialist
Group, and it explicitly directed its attacks against the
rich. The day its most prominent leaflet emerged with
the stark slogan 'Britain is for the Rich, Scotland can
be ours' against a plain black background, a startled
SNP released a press statement dissociating Yes Scotland from RIC and its abrasive tone.[21] But when RIC
engaged in mass canvasses in deprived areas of Labour
constituencies full of symbolic tower blocks and housing schemes,[22] the SNP hailed their engagement. Most
of the areas canvassed by RIC voted Yes, and duly fell
to the SNP's populist election machine in the 2015 general election.

For their part, radical elements of the campaign,
finding their demands reaching public heights, neglect-
ed the politics of conflict, and the issue of the power
of capital and powers of the state necessary to pursue an alternative to austerity were left for after a referendum victory. Where the controlled campaign was
unable to generate the popular movement required
for a Yes vote, the spontaneous campaign lacked the
skill and organisational power to remain autono-

---

21   Tom Gordon, 'We should leave Britain now... it only works for the
     rich', *The Herald*, 23 February 2014

22   Libby Brooks, 'Scottish Independence campaign: Mass canvassing
     in Glagow's Gorbals', *The Guardian*, 22 June 2014

mous. Each used the other, so that the Yes campaign gained an anti-austerity tone and momentum that took support for independence higher than ever but lacked the substantive basis of a radical movement. The Yes campaign tapped the people's message and sapped their power, shaping a passive electorate that looked up to the SNP for its guidance and direction.

Revelations

And I saw another mighty angel come down from heaven, clothed with a cloud: and a rainbow was upon his head, and his face was as it were the sun, and his feet as pillars of fire...

And he had in his hand a little book open. And I went unto the angel, and said unto him, Give me the little book. And he said unto me, Take it, and eat it up; and it shall make thy belly bitter, but it shall be in thy mouth sweet as honey.

And I took the little book out of the angel's hand, and ate it up; and it was in my mouth sweet as honey: and as soon as I had eaten it, my belly was bitter.
Book of Revelation

Ten days before the referendum, a *Sunday Times* poll placed Yes support at 51 per cent.[23] All hell broke loose, and capital, the quiet deity, making and remaking the world from an obscure Elysium of boardrooms and share price indexes, paid Scotland a visit. Lloyds

---

23   Tim Shipman, 'Yes leads in Scots poll shock', *The Sunday Times*, 7 September 2014

Bank and the Royal Bank of Scotland announced plans to move their head offices to England in the event of a Yes vote. Standard Life announced a similar shift, and BP said it was concerned about its future in an independent Scotland. Even friendly John Lewis allowed its Chair to warn that prices would rise.

It was a moment of revelation. Where capital had previously operated behind the scenes, occasionally responding to the whims of the Better Together campaign, the *Sunday Times* poll created the impetus for its well-oiled machine to hum smoothly into action. The Prime Minister communed with various business leaders in Downing Street, and the next week capital came to Scotland in earthly form.

For most Scots, this apparition was terrifying. The words spoken and the sentiments expressed were frightening enough to undecided voters, but the sheer force of angelic screeching resonated through the Central Belt and the Great Glen, and left Yes and No voters alike awed by a force casting off all the subtlety with which it had previously engaged in Scottish politics. Looking up to the heavens allowed every person in Scotland to enjoy a black-and-white montage showing them Weimar scenes of hyper-inflation, children carrying suitcases full of money through the streets, and Tennent's being sold for £5 a pint.

Capital looked at its creation, and it saw that it was good. But when capital turned its mouldy worm-infested face to the people, the people did not like what they saw. The normal functioning of capitalist power goes on behind the scenes; its extent and nature is never clear, and this is crucial for its persistence. When it's never known quite how much or how little we are dominated, the potential and limits of various forms of resistance are similarly unknown. Uncertainty breeds inaction, and uncertain action precedes defeat. But the real extent and limits of capitalist power are exposed on those rare occasions when it decides to intervene.

In the last days of the referendum certain aspects of capital were revealed which had hitherto only been clear to astute readers of the *Financial Times*. The revelation of capital's influence on state power, and its conspiracy with Labour and the Tories, exposed the intense involvement of powerful private interests in the political domain which is assumed to exist at an acceptably 'democratic' distance from the political world. The collusion of different companies and interests revealed the overwhelming unity of the capitalist spirit, and the way in which finance and industry comprise the leadership of an economic and social system. And the cherubs of capital, the managers and chairmen, board members and industrialists, were shown to be unattractive individuals, swollen with power, and creatures of flesh and blood who were not immune from a Kalashnikov shot.

The revelation of capital affords a small window of opportunity for socialists, but it also has the potential to stultify movements for change. During times of political tumult and possibility, people trained to be unaware of the real limits of action tend to pursue action in abundance. Every well-meaning citizen seemed to come up with a new, limitless blueprint for Scotland, advocating the democratic equivalent of relocating Ben Nevis to the Borders. When RBS came along and said 'Actually, we control you', most people experienced despair or denial. Everything became pointless, or everything would be fine.

The revelation of capital provides an exciting spectacle for socialists in the sense that power is revealed and can therefore be challenged. But this challenge is only possible where there is already another powerful interest ranged against the forces of capital, such as a party or organisation of the working class. Of course, no such organisation existed at the end of the referendum; capital survived the leap from its hiding-place with little more than a vague sense of social embarrassment, as if the host of a terrible party had decided at last to emerge from the cupboard in plain view of their bored guests.

We should be clear here that we are not claiming that capital was threatened by the forces supporting Scottish independence. In all likelihood (in fact, capital would have made sure of it) an SNP government would have pandered to their interests as much as possible in order to ensure economic stability, while pursuing a programme of austerity in hock to currency markets, international creditors and investors, and/or the Bank of England. Many Yes voters patted themselves on the backs when they saw capital's reaction: *look at how scared the ruling class is! We must have created a real movement of democratic socialism!* But the revelation was not a response to the transgressions of revolutionaries; it was a cautious reminder that the corporate interests of business were not best served by the uncertainties of sweeping constitutional change. Since the financial crisis of 2007, the importance of short term stability and predictability has been elevated to absurd heights. Long-term gradual political and social change hardly features on the radar of the decision-makers of capital; all that worried capital about this particular political prospect was the strange immediacy of a single day's knife-edge vote, and the unpredictability of the actions of the UK and Scottish governments during the negotiation period.

The Yes campaign was in a bind. Following the revelation of capital, the Yes Scotland messaging carried on regardless, maintaining that fairness and prosperity would arise from democratic renewal, despite the obvious and far stronger messages to the contrary that were resounding through the press. Senior strategists admitted to being shocked at the force of the attack, and gazed in confusion at the new Scotland, where power was no longer hidden. Spokespeople could do nothing but smile wanly and emit faltering platitudes like dying Furbies, as their parochial conception of Scotland and its independent future crashed noisily and emphatically around them. They discovered that socialists talk about these things for a reason.

The Yes strategists were unable to counter this force because they had stunted the development of any kind of oppositional, anti-capitalist power from the people. Arguably this was entirely sensible, given the loss of credibility for the Yes campaign that an uncontrolled radical movement would have risked. For RIC's part, beyond rhetoric against 'the rich', their activists had shied away from confronting capital itself, choosing instead to assault a caricatured 'British State' as a proxy. RIC's leaders had made little effort to prepare the ground for a coherent, popular resistance to capital, so when it reared its head RIC's followers were as transfixed as the official Yes campaign.

Capital appeared in these last days as the *only* force with any real, determining power. Socialists had tried to stow away on a nationalist ship, thrilled at the prospect of even a modest share of the treasure. The end of the voyage was so agonisingly predictable, so numbingly banal, that it became increasingly unclear whether the cramped, uncomfortable journey had been worth it.

Lights out

A whole nation, which thought it had acquired an accelerated power of motion by means of a revolution, suddenly finds itself set back into a defunct epoch, and to remove any doubt about the relapse, the old dates arise again – the old chronology, the old names, the old edicts, which had long since become a subject of antiquarian scholarship, and the old minions of the law who had seemed long dead.

Karl Marx, 'The 18th Brumaire of Louis Bonaparte', 1852

On 16 September, two days before the referendum, the front page of the *Daily Record* inadvertently captured the limits of the official debate. The lead story was the notorious 'Vow' of the three Westminster party leaders, committing to 'permanent and extensive new powers' for the Scottish Parliament[24] if the people voted No. The second story featured Canon Kenyon Wright, former Chair of the Scottish Constitutional Conven-

---

24 'Three Leaders Sign Promise to Scotland', *Daily Record*, 16 September 2014

tion and introduced in the paper as 'one of the architects of devolution', urging readers to 'vote Yes for our children'.[25]

The coalescence of the debate around 'more powers' stifled far greater questions of capital's briefly-exposed influence and saw the referendum to its forlorn finale. After the No vote the question of whether to grant minimal or maximal devolution was endlessly rehearsed in the media and by politicians. Hosts of welfare state and anti-poverty professionals followed suit, hopeful that welfare and spending powers would soon be delivered to them from Westminster. They were concerned, like their predecessors, with the ongoing erosion of the welfare state and with it their managerial roles. The class of social administrators settled back into their devolution groove.

In a Tradeston pub soon after the referendum, a socialist friend remarked on the peculiarities of the way 'the people demand' nowadays. She said that she remembered days when people would identify a problem – a new cruel form of refugee detention, for example, or the introduction of workfare initiatives – and the solution found would be to organise people to resist exploitation and build up power for themselves. But now, when someone in the pub, in the parliament, or in the street identifies a problem, someone else will surely chip in, 'D'you think we could devolve that?'

The potential of further devolution has become such a trope of Scottish political life that people can hardly imagine politics without this handy (but often mean-

25 'Devolution Godfather Kenyon Wright: If we vote Yes future generations will thank us...', *Daily Record*, 16 September 2014

ingless) solution. It is even used in situations where devolution might be a regressive move; the Green Party's principal contribution to the Smith Commission on further devolution was to recommend devolution of abortion legislation. Their justification for this was an example of exactly the kind of thinking which makes the Scottish Parliament so ill-suited to popular politics. They argued that while the reservation of abortion legislation 'may have been taken in the light of prevailing social attitudes at the time, it may now be appropriate to recognise that the progressive, human rights based agenda make it unlikely that Scotland would take actions which restrict women's reproductive rights.'[26] The people, and their social attitudes, have little role here; only the 'agenda' of 'Scotland' matters. Devolution of abortion legislation was not explained in terms of a desire to provoke public debate and transform public attitudes; but instead in the hope of ensconcing a thorny issue in the gilded cushions of liberal administrative consensus. The clear dividing line between politics and people, briefly smudged by the referendum, has been boldly redrawn.

Across the country, in the streets and pubs and public halls where the people had talked in utopian ways of constructing the future, the political lights switched out once more. A populist (bourgeois) party like the SNP calls the people into organised existence when it needs to win something (an election, a plebiscite) but a popular party relies on continuous organisation. No such party existed during the referendum, and so or-

---

26   Patrick Harvie and Maggie Chapman, 'Scottish Green Party submission to Smith Commission on Devolution', October 2014

ganised political activity was snuffed out quickly and firmly once the formal need for it had subsided.

Politics can only take place within the forms provided for it, and the form of Holyrood actively prevents the appearance of struggle on the political stage. The referendum was an unusual event in this context, because the form of independence was unclear and disputed, so there were many possibilities for discussion of class struggle as a part of politics. But this openness of form was short-lived. Back in the swamp of devolution, further changes pushed through by a Conservative majority are carefully watched by the SNP bargainers at Westminster, but all their bargaining chips are north of the border. The SNP are a ruling party, interested in maintaining power, placating capital, and influencing the specific form of their parliament and the extent of their powers and responsibility to these ends.

Of course, politics can be challenged by movements which subvert its official forms, and can be overshadowed by forms of popular organisation outwith the parliament. For many in Scotland this form was represented by 'Old Labour', an idea that acted as a placeholder for the tradition of challenging power in Scotland. The betrayal of the 'Old' by the 'New' is supposedly what left the party flattened beneath the wheels of the SNP's bandwagon on that dark September night. How much truth is there to this? Can the strands of something radical still be found amongst the entrails and gore left in that bandwagon's tracks?

CHAPTER TWO

Labour Loses its Head

*'Yes,' said Candide, 'and I have seen worse than all that;
and yet a learned man, who had the misfortune to be
hanged, taught me that everything was marvellously
well, and that these evils you are speaking of were only
so many shades in a beautiful picture.'*
Voltaire, *Candide* (1759)

ON 17 SEPTEMBER, 2014, Gordon Brown made his final speech before the referendum vote. He spoke of a silent majority, and of British institutions – the National Health Service, the Welfare State – that we should all be proud of. The Union gave us the best of both worlds: the devolved Scottish Parliament, to manage our affairs, and the strength of the British financial system. 'What we have built together by sacrificing and sharing, let no narrow nationalism split asunder ever.'[27] Gordon Brown's second coming was living up to the prophetic billing. His speech was reaching its crescendo, and the party faithful began to speak in tongues.

---

27 'Gordon Brown Scottish referendum speech', *Mirror* (17 September 2014)

Activists and advisors danced in the aisles, swaying and jerking around ever more frantically. 'We fought two world wars together and people died together', he bellowed across the room. 'This was absolutely as it was, and therefore absolutely as it should be. These chains of reason bind our Union together.' Some in the audience started to light small fires in the corners of the room and others circled the flames, chanting wordlessly in unison. Bats crept out of the skirting boards and flitted around the ceiling, looking for a way out.

'And we had another war, a war in Iraq, and in that war the bombs swept away, out of this best of all possible worlds, thousands of souls who died for a sufficient reason.' Suddenly the chaos subsided and people fell back into their chairs. They began to nod rhythmically, slowly at first but getting faster, more forceful. Entire spines mobilised to bring chins rising and falling in collective affirmation. A thousand grinding vertebrae, harmonised in major thirds, carried Brown's speech to its conclusion:

> Without the Union the United Kingdom will not be the United Kingdom. It is best that we live in the best world that can be, which is the world that is today. The short-sighted have spectacles under our system, as spectacles are best for short-sighted people. It is best that everyone gets help when they are sick, which they receive from a National Health Service which is the best in the world. People who cannot work have an income because we have the best social insurance system in the world. We should be proud of this best of all possible worlds. So today we say not that the Union is right but that it is best.

The audience surged to its feet again, seconds from its howling ovation. Applause should have exploded through the room, but it did not. Instead, every single member of the Scottish Labour Party who was gathered there together in that room where Gordon Brown saved the Union, felt their neck detach smoothly and cleanly from their shoulders. One moment Gordon Brown was staring, exhausted, at the linoleum floor of Maryhill Community Central Hall, the next he saw it become a rolling sea of faces, grins still locked in place. The decapitated bodies of the audience, showing no signs of having lost their cerebral faculties, groped around for their heads and balanced them clumsily back on their torsos. Some picked up the wrong heads, others forgot theirs entirely, but no matter. They filed out the room in an orderly way, and went back to knocking on doors and canvassing their elderly family members. At the time, nobody noticed what had happened; the realisation would only come months later.

Better (all go down) together

The standard story is that Yes Scotland ran the optimistic campaign, and the No campaign was full of pessimists. But there is another meaning of optimism with historic pedigree: that the way things are is the best they can be. This kind of optimism, attacked most memorably by the doyen of the *philosophes* Voltaire in his novella *Candide, ou l' Optimisme*, endeavours not to change the world but to accept it. As Voltaire's character Pangloss is fond of repeating: 'all is for the best in this best of all possible worlds.'

The Labour Party's position in the referendum reflected a sincerely held belief that social democracy, which seeks to maintain a delicate balance between capitalism and the welfare state, is the best thing anybody can hope for. Gordon Brown believed that in a world at the mercy of insecure finance we should gladly protect the safety net which developed to support the British people, and was put in place to accommodate the needs of capital without exposing people to the full force of market competition.

Brown was clear throughout the campaign that the welfare state had only been achieved because of the endeavours of the British people, and the strength of the Labour government following the Second World War. Brown and Alastair Darling, leaders of the 'United with Labour' and 'Better Together' campaigns respectively, expressed shock that anybody could take the precarious social state for granted. It was a privilege to be protected, not an unshakeable right with its continuation assured. They sought to dispel a widespread belief in Scotland that the welfare state could simply be restored to past glories with independence, and emphasised all the ways in which the markets (a classic euphemism for the interests of capital) could turn against any welfare state that did not have firm financial foundations.

Labour's boom years had collapsed with the financial crisis, and Brown and Darling had been there throughout the crash. Even in the epicentre of a global financial crisis they had believed that Labour could protect and maintain the welfare state, escaping the fate of smaller countries where it was swept away. Were these not the very men who had, as Brown once put it at

Prime Minister's Questions, 'saved the world' after the crash? Later they would give interviews in which they recalled their helplessness in the face of global finance.

When Brown and Darling talked about this global experience it carried an unspoken accusation that the desires of people in Scotland were parochial and unrealistic. 'What great global problem', Darling pondered, 'can be solved with independence?' Mechanisms to alleviate misery would always be at risk from global fluctuations, but social security could be maintained across the United Kingdom. Gordon Brown, the son of the manse, hadn't forgotten his scripture: 'The poor will always be with you. But you will not always have us.' The British welfare state, built to weather the storms of capitalism, was the best possible system in this best of all possible worlds.

In a different world this might have been a persuasive argument. But many people in Scotland did not accept Labour's story about the restless power of big business and foreign investors. They felt that the changes to the welfare state were part of a political or ideological project carried out by the Tories, rather than an inevitable result of government adaptation to prevailing financial conditions. The voters stubbornly believed there was an alternative to Labour's doom-laden defence of a tattered and outdated welfare system. So when the No campaign realised a Yes vote was possible despite its dry warnings about the dependence of society on economic dominion, they decided to take more symbolic action. They needed a Candide, an innocent among the people; one who firmly believed that this world, in the Union and under capitalism was the *best*

of all possible worlds and who would be willing to sacrifice themselves to preserve market stability as the day
of judgement approached. Step forward Johann Lamont, leader of the Scottish Labour Party.

The oils and incense were prepared, runes were
read, acolytes informed, a date plucked from the calen-
drical eddies of destiny, and a sacred site selected. The
sacrifice occurred on 12 September in front of a handful of bored photographers outside an Asda Superstore
in Falkirk. The green, garish Asda logo loomed. Johann Lamont stood before the cameras half-slumped,
half-smiling in placid resignation, surrounded by activists clinging to their campaign boards like driftwood
from a shipwreck: *Higher Costs. No Thanks.*

Lamont was chosen because of her position as the
spokesperson for the mundane aspects of the Scottish
people's daily lives. In her eyes, and in her speeches
and questions in parliament, every life was a disaster
waiting to happen, a constant accumulation of financial pressures, health hazards and limited experiences.
The basic point that Better Together wanted to make,
that capital's dissatisfaction would mean rising prices,
was too rooted in these daily lives to be explained by
Gordon Brown or Alistair Darling. What do statesmen
know about *Asda price*? It was Lamont's quotidian
priorities that made her the perfect choice.

Sacrifice is a social device, a means of reassuring
people that what they're already doing is *best*, a challenging but essential task in the inhumane world of
capitalist politics. Better Together's strategists were Labour Party members, sworn to upholding democratic
socialism and the common good. Yet there they were,

so obviously promoting the power of capital to dictate election results as it pleased, in order to achieve a No vote. In doing so they sacrificed their credibility. Lamont's earthy, defeated *No Thanks* was persuasive because it brought the raw amorality of the market down to the level of the people's pay packet. But it was part of a long-term loss of face for the supposed party of social justice.

Sacrifice is also a way for a priesthood to exert absolute control over its property, be it goats or party leaders. The sacrifice was a successful gesture, helping to secure the Union and strengthening the presence of capital in the Labour argument, and it also fulfilled a secondary function. Lamont could be swiftly discarded by Scottish Labour leadership hopeful Jim Murphy despite the No campaign's victory. Better Together, run with an eye to his future leadership, had sent Murphy out on a soapbox speaking tour while Lamont stood glumly outside supermarkets. But her fate on the Asda-price altar was just one of the many ways in which the referendum campaign exposed the impotence of Scottish Labour and its abject compliance with the directives of the market. Far more than Murphy's cronies had intended, these stunts made Scottish Labour dismally unpopular. Even those who had voted No out of fear of the financial implications of independence saw Labour as a pawn of government elites and big business.

The typically Scottish diagnosis of Labour's antics during the referendum would be to sigh regretfully and claim that this is the way of New Labour and Blairism, which always complies with the desires of the private sector. Old Labour apparently never had such vices, since it cared wholeheartedly about the welfare of the people. In this schema New Labour complied with capitalism for private gain, whereas Old Labour never did so because it had the collective interest in mind, which could not be met through collaboration with the ruling orders.

This distinction has only the thinnest of justifications. Contrary to this common sense critique, there was principled continuity between the old welfarist Labour and Blair's New Labour. Both adapted to prevailing economic conditions, evaluated their own power and support-base, secured a parliamentary majority and set up a mechanism to mitigate the effects of capitalism while still providing a society and workforce that capital felt would lead to growth. Would Clement Atlee have stood at the top of Buchanan Street with a big cardboard pound coin, as Labour activists did during the referendum? He might have declined to join a naff stunt, but he wouldn't have taken issue with the sentiment: of course the social state needs to be built on solid fiscal and monetary foundations, and of course we must protect whatever currency arrangement suits those foundations.

The Labour Party, and particularly those figures who led the referendum campaign were so deeply ensconced within their capitalist and social democratic comfort zones that they were incapable of imagining anything else. When people during the campaign questioned whether the British state and its rampantly capitalist economy were the best basis for the welfare state, Labour politicians' eyes bulged in their heads. The question was absurd! 'The last thing Scotland needs', warned Darling, 'are new areas of uncertainty, instability and division that separation will involve.'[28] The British state and the capitalist economy *are* the basis of the welfare state. What exactly were these people suggesting? Where else do we go?

Many in the Yes campaign thought any effort to sustain the welfare state in the cesspit of British capitalism was like conducting surgery in a sewer. They imagined a time when things were cleaner and less foul-smelling, and pointed out that Britain was a poor environment in which to operate. Margaret Curran, then shadow Secretary of State for Scotland, described the criticisms levelled by the Radical Independence Campaign as 'appalling'.[29] For Curran, all of this description of Britain as a lethal, toxic state apparatus was sheer 'scaremongering', endangering the integrity of the community. For 100 years Labour had known that in this, the best of all possible worlds, sewage was as good as anything could be.

For Labour, there was no other option, and there never had been: it's sewers all the way down.

One notion Labour

Old Labour did not openly pander to capital as much as New Labour, but it did not need to. The feasibility of the social state built by Labour after the Second World War was inextricable from European economic

28   Alistair Darling, 'Better Together', JP Mackintosh Lecture, 9 November 2012

29   Tom Gordon, 'We should leave Britain... it only works for the rich', *The Herald*, 23 February 2014

renewal, the war-time nationalisation of industry and the power of the labour movement. New Labour acted in entirely different conditions of supranational invest-ment and a weak labour movement. After the Second World War, social democratic parties like Labour had found the next best way to deal with capitalism short of replacing it. They established full employment, a strong welfare system and a state able to bargain with capital or borrow to invest in jobs and infrastructure. The social democratic idea which has persisted since then strives to maintain a delicate balance between the interests of capital and the interests of workers to share the proceeds and security of growth amongst the peo-ple. Throughout Labour's history in government since the post-war era, it has made sure that its economic policies are compatible with capital's drive for prof-it. During that era, but also under Blair, profits rose alongside living standards.

Labour's social democracy adapted to changing conditions, meaning changes in the demands of capi-tal and the demands (or lack of demands) of workers, but beyond this adaptation their central ideology has remained broadly consistent. One of Labour's ends has always been to increase the sense of shared prosperity and generally rising living standards via an increase in incomes. While in the post-war era this was achieved through facilitating workers' collective bargaining for high wages in a situation of growth and full em-ployment, under Blair it was achieved by deregulating private lending, introducing working tax credits, and legislating for a minimum wage. Blair's reforms were designed to make the poorest feel included in national prosperity; in fact they benefited higher earners far more. While in the post-war era investment in public services was funded through taxation and borrowing on the international markets and from the USA and Canada, under Blair similar investment was managed and funded via partnerships with the private sector.

Labour's ability to adapt to varying conditions is limited severely by certain economic and political bases upon which stable social democracy rests. Social democratic politics can only be sustained through periods of national growth, since under no other conditions will capital permit wages to rise. The post-war model was reliant on the breakneck economic growth of that era, which allowed for the simultaneous growth of wages, profits and tax revenues. American concerns about the stability of European capitalism provided a steady influx of dollars (the UK received a quarter of the monetary aid from the Marshall Plan, and only paid off the Anglo-American loan, negotiated by Keynes, in 2006). Across Europe social democracy was buoyed by the economic and population growth inherent in subsidised reconstruction. In the early stages of the post-war era, Britain's ongoing control of overseas colonies and agreements with emerging economies provided a crucial further channel of wealth.

Given growth, capital will only tolerate the social democratic model as long as it is determined in a political sphere to which capital has relatively free access, and which limits the labour movement's activity to the demand for a greater share of the distribution of wealth, specifically the proceeds of growth. The social democratic model needs to strike a balance between the interests of capital and the interests of workers, and maintain both within a stable political settlement that capital will find acceptable.

When this basis falls apart, Labour's social state also fails. By the end of the 1960s, with the rising power of trade unions under state-sponsored full employment, rising wages began to eat into the profits of capital. The state tried printing money to fill the gap. Political economists lay the blame for what happened next at various doors, be it home-grown inflation, the decision to hike up oil prices by the Organisation of Petroleum Exporting Countries (OPEC) in 1973, or global overproduction as Europe and Japan caught up with the American economy by the end of the 1960s. Most concur, however, that it left the economic basis for the social state in tatters.

The crisis of the 1970s damaged the social state's legitimacy and flexibility. This opened the door for the increasingly restive forces of capital, sensing new avenues for profit in the finance sector and international outsourcing, to mobilise behind an insurgent neoliberal vanguard to smash trade unions and force down wages. A Labour Party bereft of its political and economic bases was sent scurrying into the wilderness for decades.

A similar crisis of conditions occurred during the Brown years. Blair's Labour government had played social democracy from governmental beginnings to a crashing conclusion. Spending and rising living standards based on credit suddenly collapsed during the financial crisis. The bail-out of the banks diverted public money to underwriting the credit of private finance, racking up state debts that compromised public spending. There was, as then-Treasury Secretary Liam Byrne put it all too honestly, 'no money'. Austerity arrived.

Under austerity a heavily-indebted state is required to reduce its spending and to increase the flexibility and desperation of the workforce; the requirements are set by financial interests that cannot be challenged without engendering significant political and economic turmoil. Social democratic Labour has never even considered such a course of action: it would be unthinkable to challenge the authority of international organisations like the International Monetary Fund and cause concern among investors that would surely harm the people. Certain European states did try to react to austerity in this way, but their reactions tended to go awry, since they were trying to work outside the conditions set by the market and the international rules of finance. Labour's inability to respond to austerity was due to the fact that under its social democratic principles it could neither challenge it, since it was not prepared to operate outside conditions which were profitable for capital, nor could it find a way to manage austerity in order to increase or even maintain living standards of workers.

Labour's social democratic model could not implement austerity without fundamentally altering its own principles. Ed Miliband was the first to attempt to tamper with these principles: he set off to find a way to cope with an era of long-lasting austerity. Miliband didn't return to social democracy, as some suggest; he broke with it. He abandoned the idea of the state mediating the effects of capital, and instead tried to promote the state as a moral arbiter which could step in on behalf of workers, introducing legislation to give individual workers the means to improve their own conditions. Miliband's legacy was hopelessly confused, but it set down certain principles for Labour which veered away from the traditional social democratic model towards an acceptance of public spending cuts and an appeal to 'squeezed' parts of the working class that were feeling insecure since the financial crisis. 'Milibandism' took Labour away from its comfort zone without electoral success, but it did so because Miliband and his supporters knew that there was no future for social democracy in Britain.

Living in the ruin

The social democrat has been living in the ruin for decades now. He huddles there, shivering beneath rags and casting terrified glances at the darker corners of the surrounding rubble. He was the master of this place once, the life and soul of the party; a copy of Keynes' *General Theory* in one hand, a pint in the other, joking away with industrialists and trade union barons alike about the failures of Soviet planning. Remember how those corners would be lit up with huge, shining vats full of the finest ale money could buy? Now look at it: a burned-out shell, littered with broken glass and sinister dark stains on rotting upholstery. And all those bones. A flash of yellowing skull here, a fibula poking out from a wrecked barrel there; things really escalated, after the booze ran out. He remembers seeing the first punch thrown, a delicious left-hook from the trade unionist catching one of the besuited industrialists clean on the jaw. He tried to step in, of course, but things just erupted after that. *We need more of the good stuff*, they all cried, slashing away at each other with broken bottles and, after the roof caved in, bits of masonry. His office was over there, above it all, with big windows so he could make sure everyone was getting what they needed, forming orderly queues and so on. It had been one of the first things to come down, when some strange men arrived just as things were kicking off and started pulling at the supports with all their might. He remembers it being ripped from the wall with a horrible screech and crashing to the floor. Nobody even stopped to see what had happened. Men who had been willing to toast each other's health had started toasting each other's limbs over makeshift barbeques in the craters which had inexplicably appeared in the foyer. *They ate each other*. That's when the fire started to spread. The thought made him shiver to this day. We can't just leave it like this, he thought. All this rubble, waiting to be given order and dignity again. We could light this place up like the good old days! He cast around for the old cart that they had used to shift the barrels around, bring new ones in from America. Ah, now he remembers: that got smashed too. And half of the rubble seems to be gone now. Had people come and taken bits of his brewery in the night? He was still hung-over at the time, but someone *did* come to see him, offering to give him something in exchange for half of the remains. *They privatised it*. Restored a couple of the vats, filled a few kegs for a while. Now even that's gone. All of it. The good times. The social democrat drifted off, but without respite, his dreams brimming with memories of the glorious piss-up in the brewery.

In social democratic political economy, economics is ultimately about management. Keynes, whose work influenced social democrats, believed that there were certain ways of keeping a degree of stability in the economy through government intervention to create full employment. For him, government intervention was the realm of technical expertise, rather than of political struggle between huge social forces. But in a 1943 essay entitled 'The Political Consequences of Full Employment', Keynes' student, Michal Kalecki, identified dynamics of social conflict which he believed would bring Keynes' managed capitalism to its knees.

Analysing the situation of full employment driven by the state along Keynesian principles, Kalecki identified four conflicts that would emerge. First, capital would resist the state's ability to manage the economy independently by selling bonds to the public and spending the proceeds, shrugging off its dependence on the 'confidence' of capital. Second, capital would fear the tendency of the state to spread nationalisation beyond major utilities to the industrial and private sector, increasing employment and encroaching on capital's domain. Thirdly, state subsidised commodity prices or welfare payments would discredit a key ideological pillar of the capitalist economic contract: the principle that one should work for what one receives, which had traditionally held down wage demands and provided moral justification for capitalist power. Finally, and most importantly, bosses would lose their ability to discipline their own workers, for full employment removed the fear of sacking that is used to discourage labour militancy.

The economic detail here is determined by the interests and intentions of capital, and the struggles of workers to maintain and increase their rights, which amounts to a political conflict between classes. Kalecki's diagnosis of Keynesian social democracy acknowledged the centrality of *class power*, particularly the interest of the capitalist class in the uses of state power. Keynes appeared entirely naive about this. His economic theory depended on government by fundamentally *disinterested* individuals which, for the Oxford-educated Baron Keynes, would be the kind of technocrats produced by the upper echelons of the British education system. They could rise above it all (Keynes was 6ft 6in tall) and see the long-term interest of what Keynes called the 'community' over the heads of the struggling masses. The prosperous 30 years of the post-war era, with a labour movement contained in parliamentary struggle and roaring profits for capital, was the Keynesians' time to shine, but the bubbling undercurrents of class struggle were never as far from the surface as they assumed.

Liberal-left commentary portrays austerity as little more than a question of public spending, a nasty ploy to shrink the state. If only the right people were in charge, and so on. These assumptions betray a fundamental misunderstanding of the capitalist economy as something ripe for technocracy and always *potentially* free from corruption by class interests. As Kalecki hypothesised and Brown and Darling demonstrated, economic policy is inextricable from power structures which exist far beyond parliament and the administrative elite. Austerity is a situation in which

capital imposes punitive conditions on state borrowing, and in which industries and companies demand a
workforce with low expectations and maximum flexibility, created and maintained by the education and
welfare systems. Universal credit, sanctions, and cuts
to public services are not cruel punishments dreamed
up by Tory aristocrats, but demands made by capital
which states must rush to meet before their national
economy is deemed unfit for purpose and cast into the
sad slop bucket of insolvency. When austerity struck
in 2010, traditional social democratic parties, almost
uniformly in power across Europe at the time of the
crash, found themselves in hot water. Like the apoc-
ryphal frog in the saucepan, they allowed the water to
boil them alive, croaking obliviously as capital turned
up the heat. In Labour's case, not only was their previous public spending blamed for the size of post-bailout
deficits, but their ideology provided no alternative.

The last Keynesians

It was in this context that Labour's referendum campaign, and their electoral demolition, took place. The
UK party's leading figures in Scotland, and Brown in
particular, knew how dire the situation was from their
time in government. They were aware of the state's
inability to increase employment and keep up living
standards. And they foresaw that with the reluctance
of lenders and the demands of the deficit, austerity will
be with us for a very long time. If *they* knew of no alternative, there was none.

This miserable offering inspired the Yes campaign's
moral message, bolstered by the persistent claims of

the British soft left that austerity is a cruel scheme of right-wing ideology adopted by Westminster for personal or political gain. The 'real alternative', reheated Keynesianism, made its way from the pages of *The Guardian* and *The Sunday Herald* to the stalls and meeting rooms of the Yes campaign – just invest more. We need higher demand? The Scottish people can be as demanding as you like! By denying their demand for a better life, pro-austerity Labour was supposedly swallowing propaganda and digging its own grave.

Many people rejected the Labour argument because it failed to resonate with their ambitions. Given that around a third of Labour voters voted Yes, a huge chunk of them evidently did not experience the world in the way Brown and Darling described it. Many believed that any decent government should challenge those powerful interests to which Labour had capitulated. Or they believed that the world and the financial system was more stable than Brown and Darling described. And some rejected Labour's diagnosis of a morbid welfare state, carrying people in its skeletal arms all the way from the cradle to the grave, preferring to imagine a social security system that had an element of dignity about it, rather than one that simply managed and disciplined poverty.

Something else was on offer in Scotland. People wanted the old social state in better shape. For two years during the campaign, while the rest of Europe was buckling under the weight of austerity, Scotland had a fledgling anti-austerity movement on one wing of the Yes campaign. It was a movement insofar as people were moved to demand a resumption of public spending and wage growth, though it was not a movement that could carry them to this objective.

The SNP didn't advocate this anti-austerity position until very late, but they bolstered the anti-austerity voices with their simple economic figures: *GDP looks fine, slightly higher than the UK rate, and we could certainly choose to supplement it with other measures such as, for example, scrapping Trident and helping people into work so they pay more taxes.* Beyond the basic growth figures, it was all political aspiration for a stronger welfare state that overlapped with anti-austerity demands. Control over the economy itself was no central issue for debate but in general anti-austerity campaigners attached themselves to the potential of a Yes vote.

In Scotland, 'end austerity' became a central demand of a campaign which was otherwise notably moderate; both Yes Scotland and the SNP adopted enormously popular anti-austerity messages in their campaigns, but without adopting any of the anti-capitalist positions which inspire anti-austerity electoral politics elsewhere. Instead, they directed their ire against Westminster, and blamed austerity on the cruelty of a British parliamentary elite and their distance from the interests of the Scottish people. The idea of creating a new social state in the midst of Europe-wide austerity was taken seriously in devolution Scotland, because a political debate around welfare had developed without consideration of how to pay for it. Even the referendum debates about tax and spending never touched on the questions of class power that had determined the social democratic state in Britain. The managerial style of Scottish politics was perfect for encouraging the kind of apolitical attitude towards economic policy that made Keynesianism so plausible to the technocrats of the post-war era.

But the denial of the necessity of austerity in Scotland did not only help the Yes campaign. It also gave the No campaign's rhetoric about 'pooling and sharing' greater credence, since nobody was saying that social democracy was necessarily coming to an end. One of the paradoxes of the referendum campaign was that the 'Old Labour' idea achieved such prominence in town halls and media platforms in the latter stages of the campaign, even as its economic and political conditions crumbled. This occurred because there was in Scottish politics a moment of political mobilisation in which the left did not provide a viable popular set of values to be used as the basis for popular radicalism. Thus the only reference point for the vast majority of people was the Old Labour idea. In the same way, Britain's first spark of mainstream radicalism for a long time, struck by Jeremy Corbyn and his supporters, has drawn almost solely upon this Old Labour language.

The people of Scotland were whipped up into a fear that the UK welfare state was collapsing, yet competing campaigns constrained these fears within limited and contradictory explanations of the causes of its collapse. Crisis, which appears to be everywhere today, is the precarious moment between recovery and death: and the people, unwilling to accept that social democracy is being led to the scaffold, make up stories as to how it will survive. The cacophony of demands for the social state's survival have made them deaf to the tolling of the bell. It has concealed from them the causes of the crisis.

Everybody agrees that there *is* a crisis. They disagree about the kind. For some, a crisis of multiculturalism serves as proxy for racist intentions and a denial of widespread changes in social attitudes; others fear social collapse from widening inequality which tears apart 'communities' of benevolent rich and deferential poor; for others, the economic crisis continues as productivity stagnates and exports struggle; but for some this is just part of a broader and deeper failure of a 'neoliberal' economic system which should be replaced; for others, diagnoses of a crisis of politics or legitimacy take the form of criticism of the existing constitution, electoral system and political parties. These diagnoses result in prescriptions that try to nurture dying plants in poisoned soil. It's not a crisis. It's normality.

In light of this, after 2008 there only seemed to be two options in Britain, in the absence of any radical left electoral force and given the continuing strength of Toryism: either shrink the state and capitulate to capital, or complain uselessly from vantage points on the moral high ground. Many in England seemed to appreciate this when they voted for the Tories. Elsewhere in Europe, the options for the left seemed broader: the adoption of some kind of anti-capitalist politics fended off resignation to the new times. Nostalgia for social democracy was present there too, but where social democracy was more obviously incompatible with the interests of capital (as in Greece), frustration with the state of things could gain a sharper edge.

But Scotland has a particular set of political conditions in which people feel able to pursue a less severe alternative. A generation of social democrats, vague memories of the good times echoing round their heads, have convinced themselves that crisis is a passing phase. These are people, former Labour voters in particular, who looked to the Old Labour idea and voted Yes. The referendum campaign had a fresh feeling about it, but it reinforced the containment of Scottish politics within a welfarist consensus that lacks the power or strategy to redistribute power in society. The SNP and the wider social nationalist cause thrived on false memories of the glory days of social democracy. This easy nostalgia for an imagined Old Labour was parasitic upon Labour itself; sucking whatever vitality still remained from the party's social democratic tradition, and leaving it drained and pale in the ash heap of history.

Doing the same thing over

In the previous chapter we were concerned with analysing the nature of devolved politics, and we began to look at the SNP and the forces that gathered around the Yes campaign. Devolved Scottish politics developed in the context of declining social democracy in the Labour Party, and the economic crisis jolted it into an anti-austerity atmosphere. Before we go on to explore the kinds of radicalism we think can take place in this Scottish political sphere, which we will attempt in Chapter Four, we will take a hard look at politics in Scotland and the nationalist heirs of the social democratic tradition.

The atmosphere of crisis is rarely present in Scottish politics. Scottish social nationalism aspires to stand outside history, and to build a model of society that does not have the same dangerous relationship to crisis and capital as social democracy. Crises in the legitimacy of the social democratic state can be useful for socialists, and one of the most obvious ways for socialists to have influence when the state is in crisis is to create a counter-state or a people's state, an alternative type of power and control with popular legitimacy. This looks very similar to the Scottish independence project, which often pointed out the 'crisis' of the British state, though rarely linked this to global economic crisis. During the independence referendum, the opportunity for creating a counter-state sometimes appeared to outweigh the problems with the independence movement. The political and economic elites in Scotland were relatively badly organised, enhancing the radical possibilities for grasping the power of a new and barely formed state.

It seems unlikely that such an opportunity will arise again, because the SNP are now firmly in control of the development of Scottish constitutional politics, and are consolidating power in the parliamentary sphere and beyond. Most importantly, they are no longer required to present independence as an immediate and urgent response to the crisis of the British state, and far less to a crisis of the economic order. From their new position in Westminster, grasping power seems very easy indeed, and a new Scottish state appears no longer as a counter-state but as merely one more international power in a family of nations.

What we observe now in Scottish politics is both forward-looking and backward-looking. To some extent there is a return to the comfortable furniture of devolution, which was always designed to contain the idea of social democracy outlined above. But the Yes campaign has made the political sphere more tumultuous, and popular engagement is never a comfortable experience for popular parties, which must try and impose an overarching ideology or structure on the political sphere. Thus the next chapter contains an analysis of the Scottish Ideology: a patchwork of devolution politics, Labour social democracy and SNP civic nationalism, which we call social nationalism. This ideology is still emerging, and we are yet to see how far it will be accepted by certain parts of Scottish society.

CHAPTER THREE

The Scottish Ideology

IN SCOTLAND, SOMETHING filled the vacuum created by
the collapse of social democracy. Instead of letting the
social system fall under Osborne's axe-blows, social
guardians determined to conserve their society. The collapse was down to Westminster and its corruption, ow-
ing to the defects of 'neoliberalism' and the misuse of
powers that Scotland would have wielded to better and
fairer effect. The social regress since the financial crash
was a serious setback for a nation with an egalitarian
morality and a social heart as great as the Scots', and in
the face of thwarted social needs there emerged a new
popular demand for the construction of an independent
Scottish social state. Following the paths set out by Nordic guides, only the sensitive political class of our small
but developed nation could dream of achieving the social renewal their people so naturally desired.

Streams of social consciousness

So who were the dream-makers? A generation of social pioneers, who floated on the tide of rising incomes
to assume a role in administering society: managers

in the public sector and directors in the third sector alongside commentators and academics, who built careers in ameliorating social need in Scotland, and lately emerged from charitable, legal and public roles into political utopianism. This was by no means the most active and energetic group in the Yes campaign, but the aspirations of the grassroots social movement reflected their values. It was only natural that those informed about the policies and governance of Scotland would offer up answers, and that a significant part of the campaign would be about mobilising as many constituencies as possible behind the governing class: never the face of power, but always at its nexus.

Nicola Sturgeon, the 'Yes Minister' responsible for the Independence campaign worked with her coterie of advisors to carve these ideas and answers into the purer nationalism of the SNP in *Scotland's Future: Your Guide to an Independent Scotland*. The politicians who advocated the new consensus, always with the people and always at their head, peddled an ideology around the three poles of the Yes movement: party, government and campaign.

Social bureaucrats want power and control, and have an economic interest in protecting their jobs and creating new ones. Third sector managers make small fortunes from their work, and the larger the social security system, the more money consultants can demand for offering their services. But beyond purely economic interests there is a deeper self-promotion at work: the personal ego of a comfortable socially-minded administrator becomes a national ego.

The designs they offered up were ambitious in

scope: to develop, in place of austerity, a consensual agreement to provide something for nothing to everyone. Entrepreneurs of social solutions funded seminars on what should be delivered, whether a guaranteed income for all citizens or a better stream of finance for small enterprise, mini-public forums or fully funded childcare. These social architects redesigned and combined assorted models of social provision with great zeal, bringing back tricks and techniques from places they visited on holiday or read about in cosmopolitan weeklies. This cottage industry naturally led to healthy competition amongst those with social influence, yet their ambition never grew beyond the compact size of Scotland, the mutually supporting nature of their enterprise, and the scope for a concerted renovation of land and people unused to ideological cultivation.

Devolution and New Labour protected social security. These were quiet years. But as the planks were ripped from social protection, people were pressed into penury. This became everyone's concern, for if you take the nation as a whole the fate of the lowly worker is relevant to all the rest – such, at least, is the supposed morality of many in our higher classes, who earn their own living by administering and servicing the lives of those socially below them. And as well as social protection, Scotland required economic rejuvenation, a nationwide improvement which tapped the best of our resources, and made the most of our best asset – the people, the workers – to serve our national wealth, and thus to raise the standard for both servants of capital and servants of the public.

In building their bridge from the state of Scotland to

this better place, the architects and planners could only work with what they had on their side of the river. Their plans to reorder the social state were based on a series of priorities for gradual reform: balanced growth, fair work conditions, a rising quality of life, and adequate housing, healthcare and education. It would not do at all to jettison the engines that keep Scottish society running at the point that Britain's social state had shuddered to a halt: indeed the institutions of law, charity, consultancy, think tank and academia, which after all provide the nation's moral compass, needed more resources. On these matters there was consensus.

It is a comforting solution to the *dis*comforting reality in homes and streets outwith the nicer neighbourhoods: the hunger, over-work or worklessness, disease, drugged distraction, the abuse and heinous iniquity in all its forms. The cure for these ills lies with those who have good intentions, and it is they who will revive Scotland. The ideology became epitomised during the referendum campaign by Common Weal, which described itself as 'a movement for economic and social development' built on the funds of the Jimmy Reid foundation and the energy of the referendum. The paper written by the Common Weal on poverty praised the intent of politicians, civil society groups and communities but lamented that it is followed by excuses for inaction. 'We have chosen not to [end poverty]' despite our ability and means. Poverty is a 'political issue', meaning it is a problem 'that requires the right choices by our policy makers and businesses, and our communities.'[30]

---

30   Mike Danson and Katherine Trebeck, 'No More Excuses: How a Common Weal Approach can end poverty', August 2013

So thank goodness we have a moral compass to guide our intentions, so we can begin to mobilise all the constituent parts of the body politic behind the quest for better lives, so that the class that governs as it always has can take it all from here. For this class does believe in social justice. Rather than being driven by the greedy values of the British ruling class, the whole ideology has grown from a definite moral conception – that of a common weal of socially mobile citizens, giving their demands a universal and egalitarian form. The substance is to manage the wealth of Scotland in the interests of the people: to manufacture 'an economy which creates wealth through real productivity [and...] an economy which reduces inequality and provides those in work with a genuine living wage.'[31] Various innovations emerge from this overarching strategy, like the SNP's 'social wage' to grant every individual a stake in the nation's wealth in the form of free services, and further expansion of free childcare not just to the needy but to every family in Scotland.

Many sets of proposals from the Scottish ideologists are confined within a stable consensus of prosperity and fairness combined. Its exponents combine the social nationalist aspiration for a country where every individual prospers, with a conservative instinct to protect the welfare and policy structures of the country. On all sides the question of progress towards social justice has come to predominate. Haunted by the British social state's collapse and worried about the enemies of social democracy, the ideologists huddle down together in a lifeboat that will carry them away.

31   Danson and Trebeck, 'No More Excuses'

The combined elements of this ideology – social democracy, sustainable economic growth, universal service-provision and so on – form a single conceptual body, but an awkward, unstable one. It is still in the process of trying to reconcile competing desires, particularly of 'prosperity' and 'fairness', which were also (not coincidentally) the two main pillars of *Yes Scotland*'s basic campaign message (the third was 'democracy'). We can assume that 'prosperity' means a high level of national income in relation to most of the world. 'Fairness' implies a distribution of this wealth in accordance with prevailing notions of economic and social justice. These are two pillars of the ideology, but their distinction from one another poses a problem. If prosperity is an unproblematic national goal, why is it not *in and of itself* fairly distributed? Why must it be supplemented with fairness?

The ideology's adolescent crisis emerges from its need to reconcile competing social interests. It seeks to guide everyone along the high road of progress, but finds various sections of the polity tempted by side-roads, each one offering an easy downhill stroll into the fulfilment of their own particular, exclusive needs. It hopes to see prosperity pursued along capitalist lines, but this means that the first to benefit in terms of wealth and power will be the owners of capital, the vast majority of which is private. This bourgeoisie would like to claim the full spoils of prosperity as their own. But the ideology's social democratic instincts demand that a proportion of this wealth finds its way from the owners of industry into services which benefit everyone, including the workers, the unemployed and those not of working age. This is not inspired by a redistributive impulse but rather by more universalist ideas about the long-term interests of capital and society. The deepening and widening of democratic participation will empower, the public uses of wealth will enrich. The state appears to be useful after all!

The ideology hopes that the prosperity of the hypothetical Scottish state can be shared by all, and that all can co-operate in pursuit of this goal. The ideology can only escape its difficult adolescence through the state. Only if it shapes every policy put forward by the government can it draw all of society into its benevolent, consensual, positive-sum model of progress, where 'fairness' is the condition for 'prosperity' and vice versa. But this is where class struggle, that old beast, exposes the nervous, gangly form of the ideology and demands that it grow up.

Despite its explicit consensuality, the ideology comes up against the sheer, audacious *existence* of antagonistic social, political and economic relationships. It overlooks competing interest groups and sees a unified society with huge potential. The ideology condemns agitation as selfish and irresponsible: unions should resort to 'militancy' only in exceptional cases. Equal marriage campaigns must compromise with the concerns of conservative religious communities, who must in turn welcome diversity into their flock. Immigrants must contribute to the economy, and racists must not preach hatred; peaceful coexistence must be pursued for the greater good. In every corner of society, the cry 'us first!' is heard and condemned by the ideology, for it blatantly exposes those structural differences of interest that tear the programme of consensus to shreds. It responds angrily: 'Quiet! To undo these differences, which keep you all divided, we have to pretend they don't exist!'

A slogan has been developed to embody this sentiment. It came from the Common Weal project. The slogan has a certain elegant simplicity. To 'us first!' it adds just two words: '*All of* us first.' The problem facing the ideology is now relatively simple: define 'all of us'.

Coming of age

The wolf shall dwell with the lamb,
And the leopard shall lie down with the young goat,
And the calf and the lion and the fattened calf together;
And a little child shall lead them.
Isaiah 11:6

WHEN PROMISED TO each and every class and creed, prosperity and fairness must be qualified with something else lest that promise become dangerously divisive; conflict must be mediated, subsumed under something more conducive to the stability of society and the legitimacy of the state that governs it.

For the Yes campaign, the third pillar alongside 'fairness' and 'prosperity' was 'democracy'. It was democracy which would give legitimacy to every compromise between top-heavy prosperity and its fair distribution. In this conception of democracy, the formally equal representation of 'all of us' overwhelms the particularistic interests that stand in the way of progress. But this understanding of the term was as conservative as all the others: just as 'fairness' meant an amelioration of capitalism rather than a challenge to it, supplementing 'prosperity' defined as a concentration of wealth in the hands of a few, 'democracy' was not a radical conception of direct popular control of political institutions and economic ones as well. The strategists of the Yes campaign used the language of popular democracy, but by 'we' they always meant the abstract, homogenous 'Scotland'.

For some Scottish nationalist critics of British democracy the devil is in the detail: the 'first-past-the-post' electoral system is the real problem, or the lack of an elected head of state, but beyond these tried-and-tested clichés of Liberal Democrat conference speeches there was little to differentiate the implications of a new democracy from the supposed failure of the Westminster model. For the ideologists, the real difference between the two democracies, one real, one imagined, was not really about democracy in any expansive, emancipatory sense. It was about which particular *nationality* was represented democratically: from the Scottish-and-British nationality of devolution within the UK, to a singularly Scottish democracy. As if to reinforce the point that democracy must be *exclusively* Scottish, the elements of British nationality that Alex Salmond promised to retain were deeply undemocratic: money, the monarchy and 'family ties'.

It is not democracy, then, but nationalism, which provides the solution to the ideology's adolescent crisis and its only path into adulthood. Transcending the petty selfishness of sectional interest, national unity justifies an appeal for co-operation, consensus, and our undivided attention. The popular separatist form of nationalism in Scotland offers a particularly politicised national idea, and one which projects Scotland's own social divisions onto the conflict between Scotland and a Westminster elite. With nationalism, the societal and conceptual contradictions which arrest social democracy's development are externalised, and thus transformed, from crisis into opportunity. Faced with a climb to power, social democracy finds abundant footholds in the aspiring nation of Scotland, whose nationalism has plotted a route to the statehood the ideology craves. The referendum provided the locus of ideological power as well as an opportunity for the dissemination and popular endorsement of the ideology itself. It ascends to become the *Scottish Ideology*: social nationalism.

This seems at first like a cheap conceptual fix. Are social democrats not internationalists, devoted to global struggle through reform, the vanguard of a movement of nations? The Scottish Ideology has its partisans of not-nationalism, those who insist on the universal relevance of their cause and their freedom from the insularity of the 'patriot'. These troubled souls need not fret so much; social nationalism spurns the ugliness of fascism and empire. It is nothing more sinister than the endorsement of a state which seeks to look after its citizens by an appeal to their common interests as citizens of that state.

Rather than appealing to more conventional elements of national identity, such as industrial heritage, it sieves different aspects of commonality through a filter of what people truly have in common in relation to social democratic provision by the state, and the only

aspect that it must have as its basis is the state relationship. Just as an adolescent finds in Catholicism one
aspect that really appeals to them and gives everything
sense – love, sacrifice, community – social nationalism
takes the common aspiration under a state as the basis
of its idea.

But is this not just how all democratic politics
works? Yes, parliamentary democracy always papers
over social division, for even at its decisive moments,
the isolation of the ballot box tears us out of the wider
context in which we normally play the roles given to
us by social and economic hierarchy. What makes the
Scottish variant explicitly 'nationalist' is simply its aspiration to alter the boundaries of the state-citizen unit
– its separatist aspect. Perry Anderson, one of the most
influential theorists of the British 'New Left', wrote
that parliamentary democracy:

> Reflects the fictive unity of the nation back to the
> masses as if it were their own self-government. The
> economic divisions within the 'citizenry' are masked
> by the juridical parity between exploiters and ex-
> ploited... The existence of the parliamentary state
> thus constitutes the formal framework of all other
> ideological mechanisms of the ruling class.[32]

For Anderson, the western left's historic preoccupation
with parliamentary politics was its undoing; it directed the efforts of radicals into institutions which concealed fundamental social divisions beneath a veneer

---

32 Perry Anderson, 'The Antinomies of Antonio Gramsci', *New Left
Review*, November-December 1976

of equal representation, undermining efforts to expose and attack systemic inequality and exploitation. While all parliamentary democracy relies to some extent on Anderson's 'fictive unity', nationalism as an active, *political* project is only needed when this fictive unity must be asserted. As the ability of British governments to maintain the support of the British people waned, as the empire faded and the underlying insecurities rose to the surface, the British state was incapable of reinventing itself to deal with this; in Scotland, however, there was an alternate national ideal that could be mobilised against decline. Nationalism worked for Scotland when it no longer could for Britain.

The chronicles of Nairnia

The trajectory of western left electoral politics can testify to the fictive unity of parliamentary democracy, dominated as it has been by the widespread assimilation of independent working-class and socialist politics into institutions designed for the stable governance of a capitalist economy. The resulting disillusionment of western socialists like Anderson with the orthodox Marxist approach of looking to the most advanced capitalist economies to find the roots of proletarian struggle played a crucial historical role in the growth of support for anti-imperialist politics amongst the radical left. The writers of the *New Left Review* became less interested in the development of national economies in relation to an ideal capitalist or Marxist barometer, and more interested in the development of national economies in relation to each other. It was more interesting to consider the economies of colonies in relation to the economy of Britain, than to wonder how far Britain was a 'fully developed' capitalist economy. In the 1960s, the *New Left Review* was transformed under Anderson into a vehicle for advocating national liberation struggles in the developing world. Heavily influenced by left-wing anti-imperialist movements in Asia, Latin America and Africa, and 'Third-Worldist' writers like Regis Debray and Frantz Fanon, the New Left responded to the reformism of the traditional British left by seeking revolution elsewhere. This, they hoped, would spur their home-grown British working class into revolutionary life. This practice was attacked years later by Anderson's one-time assistant at the *New Left Review*:

> Who does not know the internationalist sectarian, sternly weighing distant triumphs of the Movement against the humiliations at home? His [own, home-grown] national proletariat is a permanent disappointment and reproach.[33]

The critic was Tom Nairn who, in earlier days, had occupied the same broad ideological ground as Anderson in forging one of the intellectual foundation-stones of modern Scottish nationalism. The 'Nairn-Anderson theses' on the historical development and shortcomings of the British state exemplified Nairn's later caricature of the 'internationalist sectarian'. In a series of articles for the *New Left Review* throughout the 1960s and early 1970s, they argued that Britain's culture, ideas and institutions were singularly hostile to socialist

33 Tom Nairn, *Faces of Nationalism: Janus Revisited* (1997)

politics, for they had solidified in a pre-modern era of feudal deference, embryonic capitalism, and constitutional conservatism. This had led to an archaic and stagnant social order, a philistine and deeply reformist labour movement, and an economy dangerously skewed towards the finance sector.

Nairn's intellectual divergence from Anderson following the formulation of their theses demonstrates how the left flank of Scottish social nationalism took shape during a wider, dual retreat of the radical left: firstly, a retreat from the prospect of moderate progressive reform within Britain; and secondly, from the prospect of revolutionary transformation worldwide. Nairn had initially supported Anderson's 'proletarian internationalism', agreeing that the 'fictive unity of the nation' was a crucial feature of capitalist ideology; they both opposed left-wing British nationalism on these grounds. Nairn also initially agreed with Anderson that whilst some national anti-imperial struggles could empower the proletariat, most forms of nationalism were reactionary. By the 1970s, even the red star of Third-World nationalism was waning. War and splits between 'national' communist regimes in Cambodia and Vietnam, or China and the Soviet Union, would rob the New Left of even this glimmer of hope as the dark clouds of reaction gathered at home and abroad.

Nairn felt nationalism was 'more like the climate of political and social thought than just another doctrine,' which made it 'correspondingly difficult to avoid being influenced by it.'[34] Disillusioned with the faraway utopias of Che Guevara, Mao Zedong and Ho Chi

34   Tom Nairn, *The Break-up of Britain* (1981)

Minh, Nairn succumbed to this influence, and began to emphasise the potential of *Scottish* nationalism as a means for breaking up the ossified structures of the British state and preparing the ground for radical politics at home. Nairn's transfer of political sympathies from the 'developing' back to the 'developed' world was conditional on his and Anderson's particular analysis of the British state. The institutions and intellectuals which made up the polity of 'Ukania', as he called it, were so inherently conservative, so immune to even the mildest democratic reform, that Scotland's relatively outward-looking separatism contained the potential for the kind of political change that class struggle had been precluded from creating. In what Nairn described as a break-*up* of Britain, he hoped for elevation through fragmentation.

Anderson, on the other hand, was in the process of shifting away from all brands of nationalism, rejecting any dalliance with existing national traditions and ideals as necessarily reformist. His growing pessimism about the hopes for popular radical politics manifested itself in a newfound fondness for Trotskyism. By the 1990s Nairn and Anderson had parted ways entirely; Nairn openly jettisoned socialism in favour of 'civic' nationalism within capitalism. The Scottish left's gradual assimilation into moderate constitutional politics from the 1980s onwards demonstrates the extent to which for Nairn and so many like him, resignation to the capitalist system was chosen over the revolutionary politics of former communist struggles. This position, where Nairn ended up, became a starting point for the Scottish Ideology: the Scottish citizen army gradually cast aside the heavy armour needed for frontal attacks on the established order in favour of civilian clothes better suited to compromise.

Nairnism conquered Scotland just when a more radical option became plausible again. From 2008 onwards, a wave of protests and social movements across the world with varying levels of radicalism and coherence showed the potential, if not the concrete basis, for mass, left-wing resistance to elites. Many of these protests and movements spoke in crude terms of socioeconomic division: the 99 per cent against the 1 per cent, or the people against the elite, *la casta*; even Ed Miliband's Labour Party described their policies as 'for the millions, not the millionaires'. Scotland's traditions of radicalism and trade union intransigence could have fed into an effort to take the fight to the basis of capital and elite power but instead became distant, self-absorbed and moderated by an all-consuming debate over a restatement of national parliamentary democracy.

Stars align

Whatever radical energies hid within the Independence campaign itself, the movement that emerged responded to defeat in the referendum by helping to elect the SNP to Westminster in 2015. Unlike other anti-establishment 'progressive' forces of the era, the SNP's rhetoric studiously avoided attacks on the rich in general (some Scots are rich, after all, and some of them even provide the SNP with its campaign funds). The radical edges of Scottish politics were blunted by the predominance of the SNP, while a change in leadership from Alex Salmond to Nicola Sturgeon cemented the party's alignment with the broader social nationalism of Civic Scotland.

Salmond had been a populist, but a peculiarly elitist one, fond of deference to wealthy, powerful reactionaries. Under his leadership the SNP government overruled a local refusal of planning permission to American tycoon (and now Presidential hopeful) Donald Trump's proposed golf course in Aberdeenshire, prompting furious resistance from local and national activists which Salmond and his party duly ignored. A Site of Special Scientific Interest was destroyed and working-class people were bullied and intimidated into leaving their homes to allow for 'jobs' and 'investment' which never came.[35] Before the Royal Bank of Scotland's (RBS) disastrous purchase of the Dutch bank ABN-AMRO, Salmond wrote a letter to then-RBS chairman Fred Goodwin offering to use his powers as First Minister to support Goodwin and the bank, whose collapse would later bring the British economy to the brink of ruin. And Salmond's courtship of Rupert Murdoch in pursuit of endorsement by the media mogul's newspapers was worthy of Tony Blair himself.

These were not necessary evils in pursuit of radical change. Salmond's political impulses were barely even social democratic. His vision for an independent Scotland before the crash in 2008 was for the nation to become the next 'Celtic Tiger', roaring along with the propulsion of heavily deregulated finance sectors and lowered corporation tax rates. Salmond's commitment to the model was evident even after the crash: suitable

---

35 Anthony Baxter, *You've been Trumped* (documentary) (October 2012)

conditions for international banks like RBS, alongside low corporation tax, were central planks of Salmond's economic argument for independence. Salmond's incompatibility with the ideologists of social nationalism also stems from his unpredictability; he was, and still is, too prone to bullish buffoonery, opportunistic political flourishes, and romanticised nationalist rhetoric to be at home amid the calm, technocratic paternalism of Civic Scotland. He sought to speak to the people directly, over the heads of self-appointed representatives, and was willing to make enemies while doing so, though rarely the right ones.

Nicola Sturgeon, on the other hand, is the consummate social nationalist. Her consensualism, her emphasis on the SNP's claim to the Labour legacy, and her focus on policy rather than patriotism, is entirely in line with the social nationalist ethos. Her rise to power has ensured a far smoother functioning of social nationalist hegemony in Scotland than the potential conflicts that might have existed under Salmond's temperamental leadership. When the histories of 21st century Scottish nationalism are written, Salmond's contribution may well pale into insignificance next to Sturgeon's. Social nationalism has an enormously popular leader at the head of its very own movement, with a mission, a clear and widely unpopular enemy and even the tacit support of swathes of the labour movement and the radical left. It is the dominant ideology of governance in Scotland, and its roots are now deep enough that it might remain so for decades.

Social nationalism is best understood as it comes into practice. It promotes certain ways of life, particular means of interaction in civil society, and various uses for institutions. It perpetuates myths about the foundations of what is right, constructing a story people are comfortable with, which makes them feel justified in the way they live their lives. Social nationalism forms a basis for political thought and action which quells the traditional appeal of the left and right, and fits the new anti-political age by proclaiming that it doesn't matter if we only have one politics.

Social nationalism is perpetuated through repetition, through its integration into people's everyday lives. When it becomes common sense, and when its aims are common expectations, it has achieved its goal. This repetition is sustained through establishment bodies in Scotland, many of which preceded the Parliament and provided much of its justification. The Church of Scotland and the Scottish Universities, the oldest public institutions of Scotland, are both apostles of social nationalism, as is Scotland's largest state institution, the NHS. The Scottish Government works tirelessly with these institutions to promote the limitless possibilities of universalism and social enterprise, and to unearth the assets of the nation and its people.

There are three main operators of social nationalism, who will appear throughout this account. The first is the SNP, both parliamentarians and spin doctors, whose influence in the parliamentary sphere has led other parties to adopt social nationalist principles. The second are the social administrators of Scotland. Many of these people are managerial, and reside in the public sector, the third sector and in the administrative roles that spawn from these areas, such as policy-based academia, consultancy and social enterprise. These people manage poverty, and commune at government sponsored conferences, full of hope and support for each other as the apostles of a better Scotland. The final group is more amorphous, and consists of commentators and would-be intellectuals, do-gooders who 'think outside the box' and create book-shaped plans for a better Scotland. The three operate in an equilibrium, though the SNP has the ultimate power to pick up and drop the administrators and intellectuals from their agenda. The whole machine operates in a grinding consensus. The sharp pain that Scots sometimes experience in their ears is in fact caused by the ever rising pitch of the social ideologues' highly contained excitement.

Kirstification

The entire ethos of the Scottish National Party is inspired by a little child called Kirsty. Kirsty's development as a messaging device quite clearly reflects the development of the SNP's ideas, and the roots of its social nationalism. Kirsty began as a pure economic subject, in a speech made by Nicola Sturgeon on 3 December 2012 at Strathclyde University.[36]

Sturgeon explained in this speech that Kirsty's birth place and her parents' jobs will determine much of her life. Once she has set off on this highly determined course, all kinds of government intervention, such as welfare and education, will never be able to make up for her 'bad start in life'. If Kirsty's start in life had been bet-

---

36   Nicola Sturgeon, 'Bringing the powers home to build a better nation', Strathclyde University, 3 December 2012

ter, she would have been 'an asset – to herself, her community and Scotland'. But since she was born into poverty, she is instead 'a demand – for money, services and help', 'just another figure shuffling through our welfare statistics'. Such is the binary nature of a life in Scotland.

The nation can act in two ways: it can simply allow Kirsty to be a burden on the state, or it can somehow provide Kirsty with the material to become an asset to us all. The reason we want Kirsty to be an asset is because she will then be good for all of us, 'because Kirsty will be the carer to tomorrow's pensioners and the Chief Executive of tomorrow's companies'.

In this narrative Kirsty's life is overdetermined by her economic and social position, and every individual is an intersection of structures of economic necessity and ability. Governments try to find ways to represent the people back to the people. They raise a distorting mirror that highlights the virtues and ills everybody has in common. What seems like a highly personalised politics in fact reduces people to the common denominators of their lives. If you want a shorthand for the process of representation, call it Kirstification: the human characterisation of the nation's economic life.

Ideas of society which solely concern the creation of humans who will 'fit' the economy are normally associated with a minimalist state, and therefore leave people's private lives more or less alone. The SNP's version however is highly connected with the ghostly form of the welfare state which haunts the corridors of social nationalism. Not only do the SNP represent the people as a set of economic statistics, but they are also driven to represent the people as a series of numbers about health, education and social care. This is an understandable symptom of operating in a parliament concerned with only the service-based aspects of people's lives.

Sturgeon's speech was strongly influenced by the 'assets-based' approach to social policy, which was at the time being trumpeted by the Chief Medical Officer of Scotland, Sir Harry Burns. This involves considering the 'assets' that a person has, and the 'asset' they can be to their community and their nation. In 'Health in Scotland 2009: Time for Change', his annual report to the Scottish Government, Sir Harry wrote that 'an assets approach to health and development embraces a positive notion of health creation and in doing so encourages the full participation of local communities in the health development process.'[37] The assets approach presents itself as highly 'alternative' and more human-oriented than approaches focused on inequalities between social groups. It acts well as a stop gap where services are underfunded, and as a justification of an economistic view of society. It tries to show that the perfect economistic subject will also be the perfect citizen, parent, service user.

In Kirstification, a traditional economistic model of the nation is given a new dimension. The presentation of people as assets being shaped by services and jobs and roles is not the typically capitalist view of *homo economicus*, focused on the monad in the labour market and the sphere of the economy. The social nationalist view widens the arena of the economy to include services and parts of the private life. We can think

---

37   Harry Burns, 'Health in Scotland 2009: Time for Change', 2009

about the health, social life and education as well as jobs and income of the individual in the nation through the lens of national economic life.

The SNP's development from devolutionist welfarism to their own brand of welfare economism has involved trying to understand the economic potential of the people on the basis of more than GDP. During the referendum, the SNP was trying to develop such a measurement of the economy, which would assess whether it was 'working in the interests of the people of Scotland'.[38] The Scottish Government developed 18 'national indicators', which would indicate whether Scotland was moving towards 'sustainable economic growth'. These indicators included numbers of alcohol related hospital admissions, measures of cultural engagement, and improving mental wellbeing. This new measuring device provided the government with a whole new schema and basis on which to promote social nationalism, a language of assets and burdens, community and nation, and a unified individual and national economic purpose.

As usual, the Scottish Government was assisted in this endeavour by the third sector: in 2012 Oxfam Scotland started promoting their 'Humankind Index', 'a new way of measuring what makes a good life'[39] with an evaluation system for government and policy groups based on qualitative research about what people want in their lives. The plan was ingenious: Oxfam collected data by interviewing a selection of people liv-

---

38   The Scottish Government, 'National Performance Framework', 2011

39   Oxfam, 'The Humankind Index: The New Measure of Scotland's Prosperity', April 2012

ing in poverty, and the Scottish Government was supposed to base their evaluation of policy outcomes on that data. This and similar initiatives helped build a basis for a social nationalist policy language, one which could appeal to everyone in the nation because they all understood the same 'human' aspirations.

Only the elite administrators of Scotland need a dubious and costly piece of research to prove to themselves that good jobs and a good home are important. These are the sorts of people who didn't know what zero-hour contracts were until Vince Cable noticed them, and still don't know what pre-payment electricity meters are. Social nationalism fills in the gulf between these people and everybody else, by rearranging the basis and nature of politics in Scotland. Oxfam presented the idea as fundamentally left wing, because it no longer only considered money as a measurement of the economy. The SNP cackled; some sort of miracle had been bestowed upon them which allowed them to present advanced economistic thinking as inherently *social* and inherently *national*. They were using the same old economistic index with added social 'extras' and dressing it up in humanist and holistic language.

In the most social justice-oriented of Yes Scotland's campaign videos, Kirsty was born again. Or rather, she was a foetus. A small enthusiastic foetus squirmed on TV screens across the nation, describing the two alternative versions of how her life might go, whether in Scotland or in Britain:

> 'Hi, my name's Kirsty. I'm going to be born on the 18th of September 2014, the very same day as the

referendum on independence for Scotland.
The question is, what kind of country will I grow
up in?'

In an independent Scotland, her early life would involve
a 'fairer', 'more prosperous' society, where she could
reach her full potential by pursuing activities such as
looking out of the window, eating a meal, and holding
a teddy bear. But if Scotland were to remain in the UK
she would be in 'a country that is still the fourth most
unequal in the developed world, where the gap between
rich and poor gets wider and wider'. This was illustrated by that dastardly *building*, the Palace of Westminster, someone begging, and some chained gates.

And so on. If Kirsty were to grow up in an independent Scotland she would go to school and to her
brother's graduation, whereas in the UK she would
have to go on student protests about her fees. An independent Scotland would play such a peaceable role in
the world that it was best represented by young teenag-
ers dancing, whereas the UK would be controlled by the
likes of Bush and Blair deploying WMDs. Kirsty's life
in an independent Scotland would be characterised by
eating breakfast, such would be the wealth and natural
resources harnessed. In the UK such innocent pastimes
would be overshadowed by David Cameron and cabi-
net meetings.

In short, Kirsty's life in an independent Scotland
would be characterised by family and food, two foundations of the good life (and, we assume, the economic
human asset). Kirsty's life in the UK would on the other
hand be characterised by *politics* – the House of Com-

mons, the UK government, student protests – for heaven's sake, what a fuss. The SNP were offering Kirsty a life free from politics, and full of essential human-ness, where she could develop into an asset for her nation.

The SNP aim to replace politics with humanity, which by a sleight of hand is actually economics. They try to make their highly economistic mindset seem social, not just by extending the activities of human assets to the access of public services, but by emphasising the interdependence of a national economy, the way in which one part of the workforce is dependent on another, businesses are dependent on public service provision, and national growth is predicated on the healthy productiveness of the people.

This is a new conception of the national economic interest. Where some types of national interest seem to be based on ideas of the physical stuff of the economy – shops, resources, factories – the SNP's version is much more highly personalised, and thus is becoming increasingly suited to a service economy rather than a manufacturing economy. The national interest is of course in the interest of capital, and all of these 'human' indices are still ultimately geared towards national productivity. But more so than in Britain, the specifics of the national economic interest pursued by the SNP really can be understood as the interest of *all of us*. Common Weal attribute every problem in Scotland to people's 'me first' agendas, whether that be bankers acting in their own short term interest, or men abusing women. If people were to focus instead on their long term interests, they would discover miraculously that their long term interests were in line with the long term interest of the nation. There are no such things as actually opposed interests, only misperceptions.

The SNP's universalist agenda is part of this story. People in Scotland are proud of the universalist policies which apparently make their lives much better than those of their English counterparts. In Scotland, everyone is entitled to free prescriptions, whereas in England, there is a £8.20 charge for some prescriptions, which can be avoided if you are on a low income or under 16/over 60, and is reduced if you have a long-term condition. In Scotland, university tuition fees are paid by the government for a first degree (though many students still accrue debt for living costs), in England students end up with debts of up to £9,000 per year for tuition fees alone. All children in Scotland in primary one to three receive free school meals.

The logical conclusion of universalism is a form of 'basic income', replacing means tested social security benefits with an allowance paid by the government to every citizen. Such a policy was bravely put forward by the UK Green Party for the 2015 general election, but was badly costed and proposed a very low universal income that would still require means tested supplements, drawing the ridicule of the Citizen's Income Trust, along with most of the media and left-wing campaign groups. There have been other embarrassments for universalism. The SNP's favourite free tuition policy has been consistently shown to benefit the middle class the most: the quotient of Scottish students from working-class backgrounds attending university remains lower than the quotient of English students.

Despite all this, Scottish ideologists remain attached

to the pure idea, still enchanted by its beautiful social ring. Robin McAlpine went as far as to describe universalism as 'the fundamental principle that binds Scotland together'.[40] The typical argument that is offered up when a socialist objects to giving free things to the rich is that it will all come out in the wash anyway, since universalism will be paid for via progressive taxation. In the case of the SNP's policy decisions this is an absurd argument, since its universalist policies have been implemented despite the fact the parliament had no control over progressive taxation. But even on a more abstract level, it is tempting to laugh at the universalist: *if you have found a way to extract so much money from the rich, then all our problems are solved anyway!*

Scotopia

The national interest is the carrier for another idea which the SNP are fond of, that of the entrepreneurial state. This particular idea is also a favourite of anorak types who believe that it only takes a few hard thinking men to change the world. The entrepreneurial state is a response to a world of financial uncertainty and national instability. It is an entity which can quickly capture emerging world markets and is versatile enough to change economic course in response to microscopic changes in supply and demand. The SNP's proposals for the development of the renewable energy industry and their lauding of the video games industry, which they were surprised to discover was booming in Edinburgh and Dundee, were of this nature. In the absence

---

40   Robin McAlpine, *All of Us First* (June 2014)

of the economic potential for real old-fashioned social democracy, the SNP were in a similar position to former Labour leader Ed Miliband, wishing to bypass the welfare state and find another way for people to relate to the nation. They were trying to move the idea of the state from that of a mere social provider to an economic guarantor of services, jobs and industry.

The idea of the entrepreneurial state goes a long way towards explaining the SNP's close relationship with small business. Small business is the realm of entrepreneurs, who twist and turn, rise and fall, as the economy changes. Small business leaders are also easy to placate, so desperate are they for political influence and legitimacy. During the referendum, the SNP built up a glorious idea of the entrepreneur, and then made successive small business leaders waddle out onto the stage, so that the people might be persuaded to vote Yes. The division between the pursuit of profit and the pursuit of independence was deliberately blurred during the referendum process; Business for Scotland, the group of business leaders supporting independence, did not see its role as straightforwardly political, claiming also to be 'a successful and fast growing business network'.

For some reason, Kezia Dugdale, current leader of the Scottish Labour Party, has spent some considerable time barking up the same tree. In November 2013 the Scottish Fabians produced a pamphlet, 'Ambitions for Scotland', in which Dugdale proposed that public services could be revitalised with a good dose of entrepreneurship. She proposed help for start-up small and medium-sized enterprises and wrote that we should respect 'those who choose to make their own money'.[41] Having reorganised the foundations of politics by revamping government 'indicators', the SNP wish the Scottish people to feel like they are safely in the hands of a social state, and so can begin to tentatively trust the entrepreneurial capitalist spirit which will really be our redemption.

One of the objectives of an entrepreneurial state is to make the people feel at home with business. Successive Scottish governments have adopted policies that accommodate multinational corporations like Amazon, which received credit and financial support when it opened a low-pay centre near Dundee, to 'self-made' millionaires like Ian McColl who was supported to take over the last commercial shipping plant on the Clyde. Business creates the impression that it will stay so long as it gets the support it needs to stay. The fiasco of Jim Ratcliffe in Falkirk illustrated this on a larger scale than any other. To legitimise these concessions, the government builds them into its designs for social justice, justifying grace and favour politics for the good of the workers/coffers.

The promise of rupture offered by a Yes vote led to apocalyptic utopianism from the Scottish chattering classes. Just like in the 'ideas time' at conferences, they were offered a blank sheet of paper on which to write or draw anything that inspired them. The political sterility of social nationalism, which had never been gritty precisely because so much of it was hypothetical, encouraged boundless imagination, and a whole host of ad-

---

41   Kezia Dugdale, 'Enterprise as an act of public service', in The Fabian Society, *Ambitions for Scotland* (November 2013)

ministrators who fancied themselves as social planners arose. After all, the whole of Scottish politics had been created clinically rather than arising out of any pretentious Marxist 'forces of history', so why could such a creation not be carried out now on a bigger scale?

They wanted to design a Scotland that made life good. Some tried the democratic angle: So Say Scotland brought groups of people together to play a card game that would lead them inexplicably to state design. Others preferred to use Scotland's existing expertise; the Common Weal collected papers from academics and third sector managers, before collating them into what passed for its manifesto. Still more turned to Nordicism, advocating that Scotland should copy Scandinavian policies. Two Nordic ideas that gained considerable traction were the idea of an 'oil fund', and the idea that free universal childcare was an economic policy. The SNP themselves have never been committed to the extremes of social democracy found in these countries, and their childcare promises during the referendum, which they insisted would alter the economic fortunes of the nation and its people, in reality fell far short of being a serious economic policy. Still, the Nordic countries are politically useful, because they appeal fantastically to each extreme of the political spectrum; they have consensual social policies, and are filthy rich.

Social nationalism maintains order within a system that allows some people to live privileged lives denied to others. It ignores the disruption and chaos that the wildly divergent living standards of neighbouring districts in Glasgow or Edinburgh cause – crime, racism, sectarianism, class hatred and so on – by talking only about the very extremes of inequality, contrasting the mega-rich with everyone else, or using terms only practically relevant for policy makers. Social nationalism persuades people of the value of reformism, superficially smoothing out the real divisions between classes that might damage its harmonious image. Thus, Salmond was pleased to point out that the riots in 2011 only took place in English cities, due to the strength of national purpose we in Scotland were able to sustain. Independence supporters claimed that Scotland's pension system could be better sustained than England's, because Scots don't live as long. They wished to create administrative order from 'chaotic' lives.

This all involves a haughty silence on issues related to work and the labour movement. The 2015 general election forced the SNP into taking a stance on such areas, which they responded to by silently adopting the Labour Party manifesto positions, almost word for word, on zero-hours contracts and on taxation. Social nationalists are only willing to fiddle with society after harm has been done, and the idea of interfering with basic market mechanisms brings a fear to any true social nationalist's heart. The SNP were lobbied consistently to bring in rent controls during their review of private rented accommodation, but for a long time ignored the clear public support for such a policy, insisting that 'heavy-handed regulation of rents, while seeking to tackle the issue in the short term, could jeopardise efforts to improve affordability through increasing supply by discouraging much-needed investment.'[42]

---

42 The Scottish Government, 'Second Consultation on a New Tenancy for the Private Sector', March 2015

Similarly, they have claimed repeatedly over their last term in government that government interference is impossible in the tendering process for public contracts, saying that EU legislation prevents them from cutting out bidders for public contracts who have a history of blacklisting workers or carrying out other anti-union practices.

For too long this ideology has been gratefully obscured by a focus on independence. Scottish politics and its limits have been accepted as timeless and unchanging. Only when social nationalism is granted a state, able to control the economy as well as merely devolved institutions, will it become a mature ideology, with all the trappings of meanness, coercion and contradiction that that entails.

Machiavelli said that states borne of strife and opposition will have bloody revolutions. States which were created with consensus can suffer change merely by disposing of the elite and replacing it. The SNP attempt to create a state in such an atmosphere of consensus, rooted in the certainty that social nationalism will be carried out by successive elites. Any monster with the ability to remove the elites from power will be thwarted before it raises its head.

In spite of their cry for 'another Scotland' with 'all of us first', where 'Scotland's future will be in Scotland's hands' in a 'wealthy nation' where 'Scotland's wealth can work for all the people who live here' – in spite of their suggestion that this amounts to a 'better nation', indeed will be a 'quiet revolution' – the Scottish ideologists are taking Scotland nowhere. They betray this when they promote a model where the interests of all and the interests of each will happily coincide, and where life will be much the same, but better. Starting not from the state of Scotland but from ideals, they invoke a different place to the one where people live. The only results they achieve are to inspire some with an uncritical confidence about a future Scotland, incorporating whichever audience they address into a better presentation of a future based on consensus and agreement. All their policy proposals – a citizens' income, collective bargaining, small business tax cuts, free universal education, expanded childcare, protected health spending, apprenticeships and vocational training – are only embellishments of their claim to present a vision of a better Scotland.

CHAPTER FOUR

The Underground Current

We will not wear nationalist clothes – but we will rip from the nationalists the threadbare garments they dress in to appear to believe in equality.
Johann Lamont, Speech to Scottish Labour Conference, March 2014

BEING A PESSIMIST in Scotland is unfashionable, bordering on antisocial. It is fast becoming the naked rambling of the Scottish political world. Stephen Gough is notorious for his habit of wandering through public in the nude, getting arrested and donning his birthday suit again as soon as he's released. It is tempting to suspect that he knows something we don't; maybe we're all naked, and he's the only one that's willing to be open about it. Scottish pessimists ramble through disagreement after disagreement, free from the social nationalist garments that give their opponents such self-satisfaction. They find themselves attacked or ignored, treated with outrage, ridicule and sideways glances; but they know what the others don't.

Johann Lamont was laughed out of her post as Scottish Labour leader for something resembling this. She had none of the faith in the SNP's – or indeed the Scottish electorate's – progressive impulses that animated supporters of independence. But her doubts about the SNP and independence were dressed up in a Panglossian optimism about the ability of the Labour Party – and the British state – to bring about the kind of equality that she saw lacking in the real ambitions of 'the nationalists'. Lamont, Scotland's pessimist-in-chief during her time in charge, was thus never able to be taken seriously.

For most of its history, the Labour Party has thought and behaved in this way. Their own programme, one of progress led by benevolent state managers with the support of the working class, has always been presented with an intolerant optimism. Any alternative route – communism or nationalism, for instance – has been dismissed with the kind of sneer that appears mean-spirited and self-serving when stripped of the hope that many had in Labour's own vision during the 20th century. By the end of the 2000s, with their social democratic credentials in tatters, a peculiar mirror effect took place: Labour's easy rejection of nationalism, once widely accepted by the working class, became electoral poison; nationalists, on the other hand, adopted a similarly offhand dismissal of Labour and Westminster's progressive potential which only served to bolster their domination of Scottish political life.

Labour's pessimism in nationalism, optimism in Labourism; the SNP's pessimism in Labourism, optimism in nationalism; throughout decades of back-and-forth between these positions, this stale inversion stifled an attitude of *radical* pessimism that had characterised the extra-parliamentary Scottish left for almost a century.

Don't stop digging

The English songwriter Leon Rosselson wrote a song in 1974 about the struggle of the 17th century agrarian communist Diggers, titled 'The World Turned Upside Down'. The song describes the struggles of the Diggers to reclaim the land from its owners, and their ultimate defeat at the hands of 'hired men and troopers'. The last line of the song is the chance for an enduring message, but it ends on a note of abject pessimism: 'We come in peace, the orders came to cut them down'. The radicalism of a given political project can to some extent be judged by the likelihood of defeat; the Diggers were so obviously radical precisely because their plans were violently at odds with the state of things, and they were ruthlessly punished for it.

St George's Hill in Surrey was a major site of the digging. Two of our number ventured there a few months ago, looking for where things began, and for some inspiration to take them through the last weeks of winter. Pessimists never expect much, which on this trip was a blessing. The site the Diggers had occupied is now a private gated estate for millionaires, with outdoor swimming pools. The security guards were not impressed by requests for access from two grubby youths who had clearly just trekked a considerable distance up an A-road. The guards' resolve was not weakened by the suspicious pair's claim to be historians, nor by the duo's cocky attitude engendered by an undeveloped but heartfelt Scottish notion of the right to roam. Undeterred, the two skirted the estate for an hour, before retreating to a memorial stone by the side of the road that bore the reassuringly understated inscription:

Worke Together
Eat Bread Together
Gerrard Winstanley
A True Leveller

The corruption of place by the guardians of capital is a familiar sight in Scotland. Jim Brown's poem, 'As I walked on the road' reflects on the storage of weapons of mass destruction in a country with a romantic image of the hills and glens. The attitude he holds towards the weapons is not focused on the opportunities of re-investing money in childcare and education – bairns not bombs – as per the optimistic slogan of the social nationalists. Instead, even an innocent stroll along the road must lead any radical to dismiss such optimism and a focus on the struggle itself:

I felt so sad just standing there
In a place I'd once loved well
Now used without permission asked
To house the very teeth of hell
But all those folk who strive for peace
My heart went out to all of them
Their struggle's on, it mustn't cease –
I tell you now, as I told myself that day upon the road.

The reason for pessimism is clear: the world is governed not by human need but by the protection and expansion of private property. The existence of private property concentrates power in the hands of those who accumulate and control it, and necessitates the domination of those who don't. Capitalism creates particular paths for people's lives and activities that they struggle to alter or escape, involving forms of production and reproduction, in work and leisure, which bind them to a limited existence. The closest we can get towards unlimited existence, unimpeded human life, is to commit ourselves to a revolution so that production and reproduction can be organised by the people collectively and dominate no-one. Many impulses drive people towards this kind of social organisation, among them the desire for freedom and a hatred of the way that the things people produce and reproduce, including their lives, are used as a means to profit.

Any proposed solution which is not geared towards the abolition of private property is undeserving of optimism. All we know is that the only alternative for which we have any *hope* whatsoever is one where control of property, production and reproduction is taken away from those presently in power and put into the hands of the people in common.

Once the necessity of communism is accepted, the question becomes simple: how do we do it? We don't get there simply by thinking about it. In communism, just as in religion, one finds people professing the inevitability of a better world. Their words excuse inaction. In 1649 the Digger Gerrard Winstanley in his primitive abode on St George's Hill had a series of revelations:

> Amongst those revelations this was one: that the
> earth shall be made a common treasury of livelihood
> to all of mankind.[43]

Yet, when he had written and published them, his
words left him restless and unsettled:

> My mind was not at rest because nothing was acted,
> and thoughts ran in me that words and writings were
> all nothing and must die, for action is the life of all,
> and if you do not act you do nothing... All men
> have stood for freedom... plenty of petitions and
> promises have been made for freedom, and now the
> common enemy has gone you are all like men in a
> mist, seeking for freedom and knowing not where or
> what it is... for freedom is the man that will turn the
> world upside down, so no wonder he has enemies.[44]

Communism is about shaping the new conditions of
existence. It is folly to believe we can approach it without agency and action. The necessity of action brings
up one of the most difficult questions that communists confront: how to live. Some become fixated on a
mode of life which they believe is the essence of com-
munism-in-capitalism. They individually behave and
think in a way that rejects private property just as the
naked rambler rejects clothes. Such people believe we
can return to the state of our nature if we throw off
not just our shackles but our capitalist garments of the

---

43 Gerrard Winstanley, *A Watch-Word to the City of London and the
    Armie* (1649)

44 Winstanley, *Watch-Word to the City*

mind. They reject any idea even mildly tainted by capital, to the extent that one ends up in the position of the radical Muggletonian poet William Blake who was found by his friend Mr Butts in his summerhouse,

> freed from 'those troublesome disguises' which have prevailed since the Fall. 'Come in!' cried Blake; 'it's only Adam and Eve, you know!'[45]

One can hardly have expected a startled Mr Butts to have accepted the invitation. Likewise, few will warm to those who tell them that all their preconceptions and hopes are inadmissibly reactionary. If communists want people to take them seriously, they might at least have to put on some trousers.

Look to Russia

The sort of communism we are trying to describe cannot be found in individual lives. It is instead found through the pursuit of a revolutionary situation. 'What is to be Done?' is thus the principal question of communists. In the decades before the Russian revolution a number of Russians took this question seriously. Three of them used it as the title of their books, and their varying accounts show that it is not so much the arguments as the attitudes of communists that mark out the distinctions between them.

In 1862, Ivan Turgenev wrote his most popular novel, *Fathers and Sons*. The novel describes distinctions between generations of Russians, and the man-

---

45 Alexander Gilchrist, *The Life of William Blake* (1942)

ners of the new radicals. The radicals are represented by the unpleasant Bazarov, who is described by his friend Arkady as a nihilist, for he 'regards everything from the critical point of view'. The Liberals are un-impressed by this stance: 'We shall see how you will manage to exist in the empty airless void.' Bazarov is a caricature of the coldly scientific radical. He is rude, disrespectful and undiscerning. When he is questioned on his beliefs, the conversation proceeds as follows:

> 'We act by virtue of what we recognise as useful,' went on Bazarov. 'At present the most useful thing is denial, so we deny –'
> 'Everything?'
> 'Everything.'
> 'What? Not only art, poetry... but... the thought is appalling...'
> 'Everything,' repeated Bazarov with indescribable composure. Pavel Petrovich stared at him. He had not expected this, and Arkady even blushed with satisfaction.
> 'But allow me,' began Nikolai Petrovich. 'You deny everything, or to put it more precisely, you destroy everything... But one must construct, too, you know.'
> 'That is not our business... we must first clear the ground.'[46]

One year later, Nikolai Chernyshevsky published his response to this slight on radicals. In his novel *What*

---

46 Ivan Turgenev, *Fathers and Sons* (1862)

Is to Be Done,[47] he described the lives of radicals as he felt they were and should be. He believed it was right to live in a particularly committed way in order to advance the cause, thinking carefully about your activities, and shaping your life according to the priorities of the revolutionary organisation. This required ensuring that domination did not creep into your life as it did with almost every other person you lived alongside; and accepting that the more effective your revolutionary activity became, the more persecution you would suffer as a result, and the closer the revolution would be. Chernyshevsky shunned Turgenev's description of the radical generation as a horrible manifestation of the division between old and young, played out in conversation. Instead, claimed Chernyshevsky, radicalism would be played out in real life, in the coming revolution. In its closing section, *What Is to Be Done* also reflects on how the close-knit lives of revolutionaries would be characterised by government violence and oppression. Such a life, at odds with the state of things, would sometimes be an intensely pessimistic one. Chernyshevsky wrote the novel from a prison cell, and was no stranger to the anguish and mourning that a revolutionary life required.

Fyodor Dostoyevsky illustrated better than any other writer the seductiveness, as well as the shortcomings, of the radical's disposition to reject every manifestation of moral idealism and raise a middle finger to the achievements of social reformers. The narrator of *Notes from Underground*, a depressive caricature of the kind of *new man* extolled by Chernyshevsky, rails against the

---

47 Nikolai Chernyshevsky, *What is to be Done?* (1863)

gentlemen who deduce the 'whole register of human advantages by taking averages from statistics and scientifi-co-economic formulae' and seek to inaugurate the reign of 'prosperity, wealth, freedom, peace and so on'. Dostoyevsky's radical hates the very idea of a 'Crystal Palace' which these reformers aspire to build, not so much because their attempt is bound to fail and because their noble ambitions allow them to be satisfied with the dismal tenements or healthcare facilities they do manage to erect; he hates it because it would be impossible to 'cock a snook' at such an impregnable temple of prosperity, and it would stifle our destructive impulse:

> To love only prosperity is even somehow unseemly. Whether it's a good thing or a bad thing, smashing something is occasionally very pleasant too. I'm not campaigning for suffering, or for prosperity. I'm advocating… my own caprice and that it should be guaranteed when the need arises.[48]

Dismissive of the moralists' laughter and their scorn for the inaction and vanity that result from capricious independence, the radical determines to follow his 'independent volition, whatever that independence might cost and wherever it might lead. Anyway, the devil only knows what volition is.'[49] Abandoning morality in favour of devilish freedom is a dangerous turn. Dostoyevsky describes how the instinct goes to seed if those who are possessed by it lurk underground, turning their disposition inwards in self-destructive indi-

48   Fyodor Dostoyevsky, *Notes from Underground* (1864)

49   Dostoyevsky, *Notes from Underground*

vidualism. In *Demons*, which he wrote to make fun of Chernyshevsky, Dostoyevsky used the character of an aged revolutionary to illustrate how this volition could lead its godforsaken victim to rape and suicide.

Leo Tolstoy wrote his own *What is to be Done* in 1886, attempting to open people's eyes to a terrible class war that he believed would arise in Russia. He tried to demonstrate how the state of society could not conform to a Christian morality, since:

> the existence of tens of thousands of such [poor] people in Moscow – while I and thousands of others over-eat ourselves with beef-steaks and sturgeon and cover our horses and floors with cloth or carpets – no matter what all the learned men in the world may say about its necessity – is a crime, not committed once but constantly; and I with my luxury not merely tolerate it but share in it.[50]

Tolstoy was something of a communist; he recognised the origins of oppression in private property and capitalism, and suggested that there was no rational way to see beyond capitalism. We simply had to turn to a faith residing within our humanity that humans could live in a condition that was more free:

> By affirming that this division of the factors of production is the basic law of production, an economist does what a zoologist would do who, seeing a great many greenfinches with clipped wings in little cages, should conclude that a little cage and a small

---

50   Leo Tolstoy, *What is to be Done?* (1886)

> water-pail drawn up along rails, are the essential
> conditions of the life of birds, and that the life of
> birds is composed of these three factors.[51]

But it was Lenin who wrote the masterpiece of all 'What is to be Dones', the work which a generation of communists believed had settled the question once and for all. Lenin believed communists had to live their lives according to a duty to disseminate criticism of the existing order in terms that everyone could understand, from the labourers in the town to the peasant in the field, so that all the workers could be organised and moved to overthrow the state of things. The process of organising and persuading the workers required total commitment and energetic application. Lenin was very attentive to the opportunities of his time, and determined that the moment would not be missed.

Lenin's pamphlet presented a programme that was tailored to the development of Russian society and the organisation of radical cells and newspapers across the cities and towns. It was intended to guide specific action on the basis of contingent circumstances. But, like those surreal sections of the Old Testament which offer detailed guides to the minutiae of Israelite tribal life, Lenin's war manual was debased by the process of sanctification. As scripture, *What is to be Done* had a blinkering effect on many radicals. Communism became more restricted, and critical sentiments became tied to the defence of the Soviet state.

The questioning attitude of Russians and many others over the latter half of the 19th century was for-

---

51 Tolstoy, *What is to be Done?*

gotten, as people began to create rules and regulations concerning what a communist could be, and how they ought to act. In some instances this strengthened the communist movement, where Leninism was applied thoughtfully and carefully, but the Sovietisation of the question *what is to be done?* constrained investigation into how a communist should live, and what it means to be a communist. As Hugh MacDiarmid wrote:

> Unremittin', relentless,
> Organised to the last degree.
> Ah, Lenin, politics is bairns' play
> To what this maun be![52]

Drink to the damned

Calculated spontaneity, colloquial poetry, radical elitism, organised pessimism, patriotic anti-nationalism. Contradictions find free-flowing characterisation in a Scottish communist tradition, its 20th century tenor set by the words of Hugh MacDiarmid:

> I'll hae nae hauf-way hoose, but aye be whaur
> Extremes meet – it's the only way I ken
> To dodge the curst conceit o' bein' richt
> That damns the vast majority o' men.[53]

While many parts of the mainstream communist movement during the life of the Soviet Union abandoned investigations of how an individual can act as a com-

---

52 Hugh MacDiarmid, *Second Hymn to Lenin* (1935)

53 Hugh MacDiarmid, *A Drunk Man Looks at the Thistle* (1926)

munist, the tradition of exploration was continued by maverick individuals. Scottish communists contributed to a political tradition determined to build a sceptical socialist republican culture amidst the spiritual and material squalor of industrial and then post-industrial Scotland, to take an often uninspiring people towards an untimely emancipation.

MacDiarmid and Henderson both criticised the undeserving Scots, who, though their lives had been to some degree determined by post-industrial conditions, consistently failed to live up to any communist ideal of how the people should act and bring about the revolution. MacDiarmid, in his poem 'Glasgow 1960', imagined he had come back to Scotland 'after long exile', resigned to the impoverished culture of his people:

Buses and trams all labelled 'To Ibrox'
Swung past packed tight as they'd hold with folks.
Football match, I concluded.

When it turns out the crowds are flocking to attend 'a debate on *la loi de l'effort converti/* Between Professor MacFadyen and a Spainish pairty', the dawning realisation of a cultural revolution turns dejection into delight.[54]

Henderson also railed against certain aspects of Scottishness, which he felt curtailed the communist imagination: 'the meanness, the rancour, the philistine baseness, the divisive canker, the sly-Susanna elderism, Mcgrundyish muck-raking'.[55] Nevertheless, Henderson

54 Hugh MacDiarmid, *Glasgow 1960* (1935)

55 Hamish Henderson, *To Hugh MacDiarmid: On Reading* Lucky Poet (1945)

endeavoured to emancipate the Scottish people, from the post-war era when he returned from fighting in Italy until he died in 2002. Unwilling to watch Scotland trail along a painful path to progress, which was the best that Britain offered, Henderson wanted to see a revolution that interrupted the interminable flow of history. By remaking society and culture in the people's image, he wanted to make something of the rough winds that buffeted the working classes here and abroad.

Henderson believed about Scotland what Gramsci said of Italy: 'the old is dying – and the new cannot be born'.[56] Where Red Clydeside once thrived, the declining towns still stood with nothing new emerging. And yet 'the red will be worn, my lud, and Scotland will march again' he declared in his poem for John Maclean, Scotland's leading communist in the early 20th century.[57] Bringing about a new Scotland was to be a cultural as well as a political endeavour, a dance as much as a march. Henderson was energised by the cultural and national peculiarities and characteristics of Scotland, seeing an intercourse between these and the economic or social development of history. The task of communism is first a cultural one. He knew fine that people did not speak with the words given to them by the Scottish establishment, and he sought to give them a voice. Henderson was not threeping anything down throats, but recognised that in people's national culture there is a radical germ – in the words of Raymond Williams, one of his Welsh contemporaries, 'culture is ordinary',

56   Antonio Gramsci, The Prison Notebooks (1929–35)

57   Hamish Henderson, John Maclean's March (1948)

and it is the foundation for political understanding.

Certainly there was a tension between Henderson's attachment to Scotland's cultural heritage and his commitment to communism. While Marxists are often internationalists, looking for the most universal human experiences, Henderson was a Marxist who could also speak in the idiom of the people, and in Scotland that involved speaking in a romantic national idiom. He recognised the contradictions that resulted from this stance, and the peculiar 'double allegiance' he was forced to hold:

> Allegiance to Scotland and the Scottish people,
> Allegiance to our allies in every nation,
> To the working world and the waiting people
> > Who look to the pitface
> > Where you, Johnnie Miner,
> > Will hold a red candle.

Preach profanity

We do not anticipate the world with our dogmas but instead attempt to discover the new world through the critique of the old... If we have no business with the construction of the future or with organising it for all time there can still be no doubt about the task confronting us at present: the ruthless criticism of the existing order; ruthless in that it will shrink neither from its own discoveries nor from conflict with the powers that be.
Letter from Karl Marx to Arnold Ruge, 1843

The activity of the communist cannot be defined positively since it must take place outside the acceptable critical and constructive discourse of society; outside the press, outside politics, outside education and so on. The role of the communist is therefore often experienced as what it is *not*: it is in fact a contradiction to *live* as a communist. Efforts to do so will immediately be burdened by sets of demands or preconditions for participating in political discourse, most perniciously a demand that any criticism be constructive. Liberal or bourgeois criticism exists in dialogue with the existing state of things, bouncing good ideas around and institutionalising them in order that they might be realised in all their rational-scientific glory. Ruthless or destructive criticism is contrarian, throwing out every tenet of accepted process and development.

One communist who dedicated his work to criticism was at pains to argue that criticism itself had material consequences: 'Criticism does not need to make things clear to itself as regards its object, for it has already settled accounts with it. It no longer assumes the quality of an *end-in-itself*, but only of a *means*.'[58] The critical disposition is not adopted to alter its object, nor even to denigrate it or attack its proponents, but rather to abolish it altogether. Marx was for many a destructive critic, which terrified his enemies, just as destructive criticism seems to grate against the fingers of the Scottish ideologists.

In Scotland the demand for optimism goes hand in hand with the demand that any criticism be constructive. The things which unite us are supposedly greater than the things which divide us, and therefore any in-

---

58 Karl Marx, 'A Contribution to the Critique of Hegel's Philosophy of Right' (1843)

juries inflicted under critical assault should be mended in the same movement by the proposal of a clear and plausible remedy. It is assumed that the ability of Scots to criticise freely depends on the security and community offered by the national conversation. To risk the integrity of this conversation without intending repair is beyond the remit of constructive criticism, since it might lead to the crushing of critical space.

To avoid assimilation into the constructive consensus, pessimists should not yield to the demand for programmatic addendums to their critical thought. But here communism seems to be internalising a contradiction, since criticism without alternatives risks being stranded uselessly on an idealistic high ground, far from the necessary *action* of communism. Fortunately, effective criticism already contains a sort of 'alternative', but one which need not offer advice or options for appropriation by those who are criticised. Destructive criticism refuses to compromise with all things which remain vulnerable to its chosen line of critique. Where constructive criticism offers a little tinkering here, a bit of reform there, leaving itself open to assimilation into the broader sweep of the existing order, communist criticism rejects the existing order: transformation of the condemned world is the job of those excluded from power, not those who already hold it. The role of communist criticism is to foster a critical attitude towards all the programmes of reform, revolution or reaction placed in front of it, and to transform this into radical action.

The idea of destructive criticism and radical pessimism gathered momentum following a break with the mainstream communist tradition during the 1920s. Walter Benjamin, a German Marxist philosopher who over-turned many traditional assumptions held by communists in the preceding decades, recognised the importance of this movement, upheld by French surrealist communists. In his essay, 'Surrealism: The Last Snapshot of the European Intelligentsia', he claimed the surrealists broke from a traditional practice that presented 'the public with the literary precipitate of a certain form of existence while withholding that existence itself.'[59] The traditional Marxist or communist attempts to move people to revolutionary action had, he felt, become trapped in their own rhetoric and ideas about the scientific and materialist development of history. The surrealist project paid much closer attention to the pessimistic experience of the everyday and recognised the potential for radical action based on a broad conception of proletarian experience:

No one before these visionaries and augurs perceived how destitution – not only social but architectonic, the poverty of interiors, enslaved and enslaving objects – can be suddenly transformed into revolutionary nihilism. Breton and Nadja (the narrator and subject of an iconic surrealist novel) are the lovers who convert everything that we have experienced on mournful railway journeys (railways are beginning to age), on Godforsaken Sunday afternoons in the proletarian quarters of the great cities, in the first glance through the rain-blurred window of a new apartment, into revolutionary experience, if not action.[60]

59   Walter Benjamin,'Surrealism: The Last Snapshot of the European Intelligentsia' (1929)

60   Benjamin, 'Surrealism'

How can we equate the dreary experiences people have of towns and schemes, the remains of shopping centres built in the 1990s or the dilapidated crescents of houses that stretch across the central belt, with any traditional idea of emancipation where natural beauty and workers' collective strength in production combine to spur the people to revolutionary action? Perhaps nihilism that breeds in areas of poverty and unemployment, loan-shark debt and shabby architecture can be revolutionary. Despite nihilism's depressing aspect, rooted in the poverty of experience and the experience of poverty, people's active response to their local conditions *can* shape their political rejection of the status quo, since experience is an active process. People go *through* poverty, rather than being *in* it. The life-process is conditioned by material circumstances but not condemned as a result of them, because materialism is a constant dialectic between human agent and material conditions. It is only a crass, disempowering materialism that denies the primacy of the acting, thinking, and living human in shaping the conditions of our society.

In today's Scotland, where the experience of the oppressed bears little reflection in the ideals of land reform and reindustrialisation espoused by movements and their leaders, it is more necessary than ever to find a revolutionary politics which is not based on land and industry, but on the lived experiences that most people have. Radical experience must be related to the everyday, to what is ordinary, and that means to Glasgow's ever expanding retail arena, the Buchanan Galleries; Cumbernauld's library at the top of a shopping centre; flat roofed ASDAS and Tescos; towns with a Bank, a Kirk and a War Memorial; New Towns with short strips of brown scraggly land in between; asbestos office blocks.

The furnishings of life in the central belt of Scotland are, like it or not, the materials of revolutionary action, and the left in Scotland is beginning to recognise this. Both the Scottish Trade Union Congress, in their May Day posters, and the Radical Independence Campaign, in the posters advertising their annual conferences, have used images of tower blocks striking an imposing silhouette on a Scottish sky. Whereas in Soviet realism the lived experience of the proletariat, even where this experience was difficult and unpleasant, was lauded as the universal human experience, the STUC's and RIC's illuminations of profane proletarian experience are ambiguous and surreal: experience is recognised as the basis of action, even if the experiences in question are uninspiring.

Socialists who tend to resort to abstract terms when discussing politics have difficulty representing the struggle using images of everyday life. Benjamin believed that despite the difficulties this was what a communist needed to do if they were to convert their pessimism into action: 'to organise pessimism means nothing other than to expel moral metaphor from politics and discover in political action a sphere reserved 100 per cent for images.'[61] At the closing speech of the Radical Independence Conference in 2013, Cat Boyd quoted Jimmy Reid: 'The untapped potential of our North Sea oil is nothing to the untapped potential of our people.' The metaphor obscures the meaning: ma-

61   Benjamin, 'Surrealism'

terial potential and human potential are uncritically mixed, and struggle and experience are hidden. Jimmy Reid used his experience of historic events of the struggle – the UCS work-in and the Clydeside decline – to endeavour to make the people into the organs of the nation by promoting an abstract ideal of inherent human worth. Marx attacked this socialism of 'man as such', detached from working-class people in their real historical and social context. With his vague humanism, Jimmy Reid, whose oratory used metaphor to describe the condition of alienation ('the rat-race is for rats – we are not rats'),[62] departed from experiences of those individuals and families who, formerly involved in struggle, now lived in a post-industrial environment. He embarked on a journey of ideas which took him far from an understanding of the sort of revolutionary action that could be undertaken by the existing working class.

So how can we account for the way in which the referendum left held the two concepts, moral metaphor, as in Reid's often-quoted speeches, and profane illumination, as in RIC's representation of tower blocks, together as part of one movement? Crudely, because the referendum was a nauseating moment of 'working together', two left tendencies converged. One was an older generation, schooled in the moral response to Thatcherism, the other a younger left which was in many ways more diverse and responsive to experiences of today's conditions. This disjoint is also represented in the trade union movement, and particularly in Unite the Union, torn between giving greater weight to youth

62 Jimmy Reid, *Rectorial Address at Glasgow University* (1971)

organising and community organising focussing on precarious work and the experience of zero-hours contracts, and holding on to its traditional links to heavy industry. The young left is trying to articulate experience, and it struggles most when wedded to the older left. This older left undoubtedly cares about the experience of workers in the new labour market and new living conditions, but they treat these conditions as abnormal, amoral intrusions into a traditional labour market of stable and secure terms and conditions: they do not experience these conditions as normality, and they refuse to believe that crisis is the order of the day.

The cunning of treason

When the country in which I had just set my foot was set on fire about my ears, it was time for me to stir, it was time for every man to stir.
Thomas Paine, *Common Sense*

The question for the young left remains the same as it has always been. Given the potential for a radical reaction to experience, given the possibility of an organised pessimism, how can we reach a situation where power can be redistributed from the rulers to the oppressed? Far from the fertile ground of experience, most communists sit shivering at each pole of the left: Euro-communism advocates the creation of broad-based social movements to win parliamentary power, and Labourism relies on the Party of those parts of the working class privileged enough to be neatly organised to achieve the same. People in both groups have become entranced by a questionable reading of Antonio

Gramsci, which claims that the work of the socialist is to build up *counter-hegemony*. They are interested in a legitimate socialist ideology, a deeply felt social morality, and the politics of the movement. But all forms of movementism carry people away, often to disappointing horizons.

We are more interested in power than legitimacy, more interested in experience than ideology. When people are organised and claiming control, when socialist cadres have understood and responded to experience, then they might think about legitimacy and ideology. Socialists should seek the support of the people, and pursue democracy as the only means to ensure practice is linked with experience. But the support and democracy they seek should not be based on the legitimacy of bourgeois parliamentary democracy or the whims of the media. Instead, support should be based on the desire for power held by the oppressed, democracy should be the emancipatory means of pursuing action based on experience. The socialist uses for ideology and legitimacy remain slim.

Power serves the people. At the moment of crisis and in the last instance (the two most important political moments), power may trump the bland ideology peddled by the political classes. The full strength of the SNP's Yes ideology, which won them a record-breaking vote in the general election, failed to win out over the voice of capital before the referendum. Similarly, the Scottish Ideology is so very effective under devolution because there are so few interests wielding power against the operators of the Scottish Parliament. Scotland was carried away by ideology, which concerns itself more with inaction than action – it places the people in a state of suspension where they are not fighting for or against capitalism. For all these reasons, power, not legitimacy, is the goal of the socialist.

It *is* necessary to attack the ideology of the SNP, and to explore it thoroughly, for the first step when claiming power is drawing lines, taking sides, being able to identify the enemy. Organisations like the Radical Independence Campaign and the Scottish Socialist Party built movements they hoped would carry the left into positions of influence, where they would have the kind of public platform to advocate policies to redistribute wealth and power. This tactic is unsuited to the Scottish atmosphere. There is already a stable, broad-based social nationalist consensus in Scotland behind the SNP, dominated by the conservative idea of progress. This conformism cannot be hijacked in the name of radicalism, as some hoped it could in the aftermath of the referendum. Instead, it needs to be interrupted, broken down into its constituent interests, and ultimately divided along clear, bold lines of exploiters against exploited, powerful against powerless. It cannot be 'all of us first'.

To reach a situation of mass empowerment, one step for socialists is to seize the power of the state, or at least elements of the state apparatus (including parties, social institutions, universities etc.). They might do this through smaller political parties, trade unions or clandestine cadres, but in any case it is necessary to follow certain principles for action. Socialists should seize power through treason, interruption and mutiny.

We shouldn't forget the legacy of treacherous radicals like Tom Paine, who used treason consistently as a tactic against all who wielded power against the people, starting with his own monarch. Paine careered around the world writing pamphlets against the entire system of hereditary rule. He recognised that treason against one sovereign was not enough since the leaders of Europe were in conspiracy. Paine taught that if treason were to be adopted as a principle for radicals it could guide fast-paced action across the board.

Paine was a radical *par excellence*, with a relentless spirit, who let his instinct for action override his doubts about the revolution's success. Charged with treason in Britain, he fled to France, where he was elected to the revolutionary National Convention. Soon he was required to take a side on whether Louis Capet (crowned Louis XVI) should be tried for his part in trying to usurp the revolutionary government. His attitude was that the revolutionaries should strike wherever they could reach, always conscious of the importance of one action in the international struggle. In his speech to the Convention, he described the conspiracy of monarchs and the opportunities of treason:

> There was formed among the crowned brigands of Europe a conspiracy which threatened not only French liberty, but likewise that of all nations. Everything tends to the belief that Louis XVI was the partner of this horde of conspirators. You have this man in your power, and he is at present the only one of the band of whom you can make sure.[63]

63   Tom Paine, 'On the Propriety of Bringing Louis XVI to Trial', 21 November 1792

The spirit of treason needs to be carried through right to the end, and revolutionaries should not risk delay nor let public opinion obstruct their goal. The traitor commits the ultimate crime against the sovereign, and has a clear eye on what they wish to abolish. Treason is a form of violence against the state which is generally presented as an attack on the people. This was true when a monarch reigned. It is even truer now that parliamentary democracy maintains the illusion of popular control. Democrats claim that the will of the people-in-parliament is inviolable, and so the parliament is used as a shield against attack on the interests it protects. The traitor attacks the appearance of this new kind of sovereign, and must thereby also attack those who claim to represent the people.

Today, legitimacy is presumed to lie with the 'sovereign will of the Scottish people', represented by the only people who ever seem to use that phrase: the politicians in the SNP and their supporters in the media. SNP politicians hold up the idea like a mirror and hide behind it. The people see only themselves, not the rulers hiding behind the glass. Treason means attacking your own reflection and smashing this mirror, breaking apart the image of the Scottish people that the SNP have created. To undermine the Scottish government and interrupt the steady rise of social nationalism radicals must use all the cunning of treason to expose and then assail the interests that rule in Scotland, not sparing those parts that the public are convinced represent them.

It is necessary to strike only at crucial moments when the dominance that capital has in normal circumstances is exposed. The experience of capital's real power exercised in and through the state can break apart the image of a unified, 'represented' people. It exposes politics as a clash of material interests rather than ideas. Real exposition and criticism changes image into experience. In order to use moments when elemental forces rush through the ideal plane of politics – when huge multinationals dictate policy to government or frighten the people, when international financial institutions override popular votes – the socialist requires an understanding of where power lies, what sort of events will cause weakness or force power to expose itself, and which kinds of events may unleash 'roch winds'. The tools of criticism need to be cultivated through examination of power and history, and exploration of the contradictions in every situation. It means, for instance, studying and illuminating the contradiction between the pro-democracy narrative of the European Union and the cruel technocracy of its power in Greece. When an opportunity arises to expose the forces behind the state, which tends to happen during periods of economic or political crisis, it is incumbent on socialists to use these moments to subject capitalist power to a glaring scrutiny.

Crisis is merely a moment of intense difficulty and danger for the ruling class, which employs all its skill and force to bring the situation back under control. Radicals have to deal with the crisis more expertly than those who wish to manage it, deploying guile to take control of fortune. At this point of grappling for power, the focus for radicals should not be on winning the support of the people (which is not the focus of the elites at moments of crisis) but on taking stock of the support and power they have and deploying it against the power of the elites. The support of the people may be a by-product of this action, but it is not the goal. The goal instead is to create a situation where the people have power. Socialists should organise for moments like this in order to interrupt the expected resolution of crisis. Outside periods of crisis they should build the forces and resources to respond to the signs of crisis and the manoeuvres of the ruling class. They must rail against the idea of *progression* towards socialism: progress is used as a byword for stability by those determined to prevent a rupture. Progress has no place for socialists, and socialists have no use for progress.

Why can socialism not take a longer, more transparent approach of building support to take seamless control of the state from those who control it? The answer is to do with the strength of the ruling powers, who use media, policy and threats to keep the people in awe, presenting their own rule as the necessary order. Socialists are incapable of presenting their approach as *more* orderly, or more in keeping with the expected course of history. Radicals must follow a process of perception and positioning, shadowing and often occupying positions that give insight into the process of government or capitalist tactics, before the moment of interruption. This approach jars with socialists who see their project as leading the gradual march of history, who believe they are promoting a certain truth of how humans can best work together and save the planet. Their enemies in parliament and in business do not recognise such lumbering truths, and are not weighed down by an idea of history; instead they pursue the blind motive of indiscriminate profit. They are light-footed, flexible, and will nearly always triumph against a snail-paced socialist machine.

General and all-out assault will make little impact on a well-armoured establishment. The moments of weakness come when parts of the armour have to be replaced and the body of the state is exposed in response to or in preparation for the transfer of powers, a change of government, a change of leader, or constitutional events like referenda. Rather than allowing the political elite to ride comfortably through political transitions, the left in Scotland needs to look for moments when it can create an atmosphere of turmoil and tumult with which those who control the state will struggle to cope. At that stage the time is ripe for mutiny. The traitors should gather, recognise the moment, and begin to act in concert. Until that point, socialists must bide their time, preparing for any disruption in the course of politics, and infiltrating the control-rooms and distribution-points of the state apparatus.

In making sense of this mutinous approach, there is something to be learned from the tactics of Long John Silver. In Robert Louis Stevenson's *Treasure Island*, Long John boards the ship in the guise of a quartermaster, and brings with him most of the crew. When they approach Skeleton Island, Long John and his band of mutineers choose the optimal moment to take over the mission. Hijacking the ship of state for the ends we will now describe demands preparation and readiness for that moment of vulnerability in the rulers and weak confidence amongst the crew.

The opportune moment during the referendum

was described earlier as the revelation, when capital showed its face to a population that were being carried away by the SNP's ideal offer. This was the point at which the traitors for Yes, who had been biding time, working in the Yes campaign, waiting for the moment of interruption, should have mutinied. They should have used the inaction of the SNP in the face of capital to expose the SNP's lack of power against this larger enemy, and demonstrate the fawning complicity of Salmond with the demands and diktats of RBS and Lloyds TSB, and his attempt to counter the onslaught by rallying his own set of business leaders.

In moments like these, left parliamentarians need to raise their pitch, suddenly demanding the impossible. Movements for specific policies need to shift from lobbying and organising towards direct action like occupations, strikes and protests. Trade unions need to ramp up the militancy of workers, demanding that the state take their side against capital. A hitherto hidden, bunkered cell of radicals needs to bring this sudden chaos into fruition.

The three moments of radical action are therefore treason, interruption, and mutiny. Treason is the will to act against one's sovereign, the determination to betray it, and the understanding that only by its overthrow can the order be replaced; it is the understanding that every particular action against a sovereign is part of the general movement against the ruling class. Interruption takes place in a carefully chosen moment of crisis, when exposition and swift action change the expected course of events. Mutiny is the moment when your forces act, when actual power is brought to bear.

In order to achieve the mutiny we describe, radicals must undermine the legitimacy of the ruling class. This activity involves changing people's perceptions and experiences of the whole political sphere and the way economic and social power is used in civil society. Because this kind of activity challenges the basis of power itself, the mutinous radical operates in an arena of delegitimised politics.

In these situations the illegitimacy of the ruling class is not so much caused by their actions as by the changed attitude of the people towards power: in minor disruptions people will view elections or economic policy differently, whilst in major disruptions, such as revolts and revolutions, even forms of economic exchange or social control disintegrate in the face of lawlessness and looting. In such a situation, the rulers and the usurpers alike come under increased scrutiny from all sides, and radicals often struggle to give themselves an air of legitimacy that they can wield against the ruling class. The left's endeavour for legitimacy seems like a radical course of action at the time, but is rarely a useful political tactic: the successful 'Oxi' vote in Greece quickly degenerated into chaos, since in the last instance legitimacy played very little part in the power the Greek government could wield against global capital. Radicals must act in the knowledge that the raw power of capital trumps legitimacy bestowed by democratic processes and principles.

Niccolò Machiavelli was concerned with the question of how to act in times of political illegitimacy. He described how throughout Florentine and Roman history, potentially seamless successions had been spoilt by chancers who seized the moment. These people were then cast into a delegitimised political sphere. The moment of mutiny, when these wily and treacherous figures seized control, was necessarily the *peak* of their power. From that point on, time would be against them. Every passing hour allowed their enemies to consolidate their power and overcome the emergency or crisis, while the power of the usurpers waned. As Han Solo said: 'The longer we're here the less luck we're gonna have.'[64] The question for communists is whether they can usefully act in a situation of delegitimised politics without primarily aiming to gain legitimacy.

Throughout this process, communists should avoid obsession with controlling the government to the point of excluding consideration of other parts of the state. The state is not as unitary as its governors would have us believe; the moment socialists assume power the unitary nature disintegrates, and the organs of state are disparate. It is necessary therefore to enter into different parts of the state: media, universities, economic bodies, public services, etc. Like Long John Silver's crew, in the quiet part of the journey communists need to infiltrate and take a well-placed role in operation of different aspects of the state. They will be there when the opportunity arises for action. Trade unionism provides the organisational basis for this strategy, operating in every part of society except the army. Mostly trade unions react to capitalism and keep it as good as possible. Under the crisis we describe they can act in a dual relationship with those who are attempting to control the state, both giving and receiving power.

64 *Star Wars: The Force Awakens* (2015)

The socialist who struggles for legitimacy once in power is fighting a losing battle, since the tools of legitimacy are much harder to grasp than the levers of state. Once in power the priority for radicals may not be holding onto support or preserving their own power but instead might involve doing what should be done to sharpen the struggle between the people and their rulers, who are as strong as ever in the extra-political sphere. Machiavelli said that 'the gulf between how one should live and how one does live is so wide that a man who neglects what is actually done for what should be done learns the way to self-destruction rather than self-preservation'.[65] If communists are interested in what should be done they must sacrifice self-preservation in favour of self-defeat, and they must sacrifice legitimacy in favour of bringing power to the people in fast and effective action.

One way or another, if socialists have an impact they will provoke the kind of response either internally or from international powers that will always make their own defeat the most likely outcome. And therefore their legacy can never be a utopian society, transformed according to schemes and policies built on a theoretical foundation. Instead they have the potential to introduce a new stream of agitation and an instinct for freedom that is unpredictable and cannot be controlled. The attitudes we have described towards seizing the state – interruption, mutiny, treason – should not cease when the state has been taken. They should be magnified. A socialist state should not try to resolve struggle; it should take sides in domestic and interna-

65   Niccolò Machiavelli, *The Prince* (1513)

tional struggle, and push forward to the next confrontation. In place of resolution, there must be ongoing revolution.

The blowout

The politics of class, of revolution, of socialism, have been forced underground. There are cracks in the image of society offered to us by the ruling class – poverty in the absence of scarcity, violence in the absence of war, oppression in the absence of tyranny – and they are pushed apart by a forgotten force. In an introduction to a collection of Benjamin's essays, Hannah Arendt compared his method of criticism to the way that 'one obtains water by drilling for it from a source concealed in the depths of the earth.'[66] The task of the radical historian, Benjamin suggested, was to break apart the conservative image of history as progress. The only kind of force which could make real progress was one which knew it was likely to lose: 'there is nothing which has corrupted the German working class so much as the opinion that *they* were swimming with the tide.'[67] But where optimism leads to complacency, pessimism can lead to resignation. It is, after all, hard to ignore the fact that 'the tradition of the oppressed' is by definition a tradition of one catastrophic defeat after another. And yet it was the efforts of the oppressed to fundamentally alter their condition that interrupted the fiction of progress; they sought to 'explode the con-

---

66   Hannah Arendt, 'Introduction' to Walter Benjamin, *Illuminations* (1968)

67   Walter Benjamin, *On the Concept of History* (1940)

tinuum of history' by drawing on those memories of defeat and oppression which made them rage against those in power.

This idea of history would not be mere nostalgia; it would be a real political force, driven by anger, missionary zeal and the hope of redemption. Hannah Arendt's reading of Benjamin was too environmentally friendly – he wasn't drilling for water, he was drilling for *oil*. Oil is the earth's underground history, a fossil fuel of forgotten flora and fauna. Drill into it at a certain point, however, and it might erupt in a tower of flame. One such 'blowout' is described thus:

> With a roar like a hundred express trains racing across the countryside, the well blew out, spewing oil in all directions... The derrick simply evaporated. Casings wilted like lettuce out of water, as heavy machinery writhed and twisted into grotesque shapes in the blazing inferno.[68]

Governments seek to avoid the blowout at all costs, erecting oil rigs that burn a slow stream of the energy of the people – not too little, not too much, just enough to show them that they have the balance right. Radical politics looks for a forgotten, marginalised force, suddenly endowed with violent power by an exploration into its depths. Socialists go looking for the blowout, igniting the oil that keeps capitalism moving: the underground energy of the working class.

Throughout our criticism of many parts of Scottish

---

68 'Ending Oil Gushers – BOP', American Oil and Gas Historical Society, July 2003

politics, our intention has always been to strengthen the radical left, in order that it can successfully bring power to the people through disruption that seeks to make *mair nor a roch wind* of the crises that sweep the state. And though we are pessimistic about many ideas just as Robert Louis Stevenson was when he criticised the 'little, peering, partial eyesight of men',[69] we are profoundly optimistic about the potential for communist action. Stevenson felt that despite their delusions of grandeur, young revolutionaries were just as right and just as wrong as their elders:

> When the torrent sweeps the man against a boulder, you must expect him to scream, and you need not be surprised if the scream is sometimes a theory... But it is better to be a fool than to be dead. It is better to emit a scream in the shape of a theory than to be entirely insensible to the jars and incongruities of life and take everything as it comes in a forlorn stupidity. Some people swallow the universe like a pill; they travel on through the world, like smiling images pushed from behind.[70]

One way or another, if socialists are to have an impact they will provoke the kind of response, either internally or from international powers, that will always make defeat the most likely outcome. Scottish communism is young. It wants to haul down the structures that keep the world in awe to capital. It wants to burst social nationalism's ballooning inventions, which burn the po-

69   Robert Louis Stevenson, *Crabbed Age and Youth* (1907)

70   Stevenson, *Crabbed Age and Youth*

litical energies of the people and lift them away on a foolish ride far above a blighted land. For it is better to be invigorated by theory than uplifted by theology. Better to harness the roch wind than let it carry you away.

Unparliamentary Language

The real business of Socialists is to impress on the workers the fact that they are a class, whereas they ought to be Society; if we mix ourselves up with Parliament we shall confuse and dull this fact in people's minds instead of making it clear and intensifying it. The work that lies before us at present is to make socialists, to cover the country with a network of associations who feel their antagonism to the dominant classes, and have no temptation to waste their time in the thousand follies of party politics. If by chance any good is to be got out of the legislation of the ruling classes, the necessary concessions are much more likely to be wrung out of them by fear of such a body, than they are to be wheedled and coaxed out of them by the continual life of compromise which 'Parliamentary Socialists' would be compelled to live, and which is deadly to that feeling of exalted hope and brotherhood that alone can hold a revolutionary party together.

William Morris, in 'Socialism and Politics', *Commonweal*, July 1885

THE AFTERMATH OF the referendum campaign was a time of political exhaustion for campaigners and a large fraction of the Scottish population. The 2015 elections had brought both depression and glee: exhilaration at making such an offensive gesture as to send 56 SNP MPs to Westminster was dampened by the terrible certainty of five more years of Tory rule. A shameless Jim Murphy clung to his post as Scottish Labour leader, only eventually agreeing to step down on the condition he could stay a month to have a square go at the trade unions.

In the wake of the referendum No vote and the Tory majority, socialism reared its head again. Jeremy Corbyn, an outsider in the parliamentary party who barely managed to achieve the number of MPs' nominations required to get on the Labour leadership ballot paper, made a startling rise to the surface via an intensely popular leadership campaign and the signing up of new members and supporters to the Labour party. Corbyn is the most anti-establishment British opposition party leader in history. His political sympathies are rightly considered to be a threat to the existing national and international order.

From the point of view of the right-wing press, the support for Jeremy Corbyn generated inside and outwith the Labour party was comparable to the SNP's dominance through the referendum: a monstrous result of popular power, in defiance of carefully cultivated public ideology and political orthodoxies. Given the proximity of the rise of the independence movement with Corbyn's political success it is not surprising that the two events are compared. After all, how can these two moments, unheard of in the history of Britain, have taken place in the time span of a year, and not have some relationship? And yet, from the Scottish perspective, the two events felt decades apart.

The Scottish public's cynicism about Labour seemed irreversible: nothing was going to persuade Scots to take a British Labour road to a better future. Scotland was no country for old socialists. A Radical Independence Campaign organiser insisted 'there cannot be a Corbynist Labour Party in Scotland' because 'the social resources needed to achieve this are terminally alienated from Scottish Labour'.[71] Corbyn was a story the radical independence generation didn't want to know.

Across the UK Corbyn's victory hinged on two generations. The first was a young cohort, veterans of the 2011 protests, school-kids radicalised by local anti-austerity campaigns and folk who learned their socialism from new social networks. These activists were much of the driving force behind Corbyn's grassroots campaign, and they are the main target of Momentum, the extra-parliamentary (and technically non-Labour Party) campaign to make Corbyn's impact as wide as possible. The other generation is much more traditional, comprising stalwarts of the Labour left, some of whom left the party over Iraq and know the mechanisms and networks of the party well.

The Corbyn campaign in Scotland did not give credit to the post-referendum instincts of the independence generation. The public message was an unreformed re-

---

71 Jonathan Shafi, 'Why there cannot be a Corbynite Labour Party in Scotland', *Bella Caledonia*, 18 September 2015

statement of No-campaign propaganda. Senior figures in the Labour left in Scotland fed Corbyn the same tired mantra they had used during the referendum, citing the commonality of the working class across Britain as an argument for constitutional stability. Corbyn obligingly trotted this line out when he was asked a question about independence at his Dundee election event:

> 'I was told by Alex Salmond and others that this was a once in a lifetime or once in a generation opportunity, I can't remember the exact –'
>
> (Audience Member) '– It's no up to him.'
>
> 'I realise it's not up to him but I'm saying he is somebody that said that... it's also about solidarity of what we do. If you're poor and you're unemployed and you're living in bad housing in Dundee, in Aberdeen, in Glasgow, or Birmingham, or Manchester, or London, you're still poor and living in bad housing and unemployed.'

The thousand-strong Corbyn rally in the Glasgow Fruitmarket on 14 August was the high-water mark of Labour radicalism since devolution in a very shallow pool of Scottish Labour leftists. Where Corbyn's rallies in London and across England brought in diverse community activists and campaigners to tell their experiences to packed auditoriums, the Scottish campaign was tightly controlled. Organisers were well aware that grassroots activism in Scotland was overwhelmingly pursued by Yes activists, whereas Labour had lost all of its community roots. Accordingly, Corbyn's Glasgow rally was addressed by a series of past, present and future Labour politicians. Corbyn held the audience's attention with a speech founded on the kind of moral imperatives that characterised the old Independent Labour Party: we as a society must provide for the hungry and the homeless, cherish our children, learn to protect the planet, and abolish the atomic bomb before it's too late. With this limp offering he failed to reform the stale image of post-No Scottish Labour.

But Corbyn's Scottish allies *could* revive a tradition that can inject a new kind of struggle into a politics stultified by social nationalism. Labour should not limit itself to acting through parliament but should also act through the extra-parliamentary combination of those committed to replacing this system with another. It is not just the size of these associations' membership that is important, but the revolutionary activity which can expose the conflicting interests of the majority of people and the ruling order. Class conflict happens all the time, but is kept within safe boundaries. We need more than parliamentary socialism.

The Labour Party started life in 1900 as the Labour Representation Committee, the parliamentary arm of collective labour organisations that held power in the economy and society and sought to win certain gains – workers' rights, voting rights and so on, through parliament. Those original Labour representatives in the House of Commons saw the parliament not as a senate for advising the government but as one assembly for challenging it; not as a balancing power to restrain the ruling class but as a chain to hold it back from terrible actions; not as a place for compromises but a place to expose the twisted ambitions of capital. It was just one tactic in a suite of strategies for challenging class power: it came out of the movement to improve popular conditions.

This tradition always has insisted that to defy capital's domination the battle must be fought in the economy, in the streets and in communities. John McDonnell, the shadow chancellor who cited Mao in his response to the Tory Budget, has always insisted that industrial action can be used to political ends: labour's conflict with the state builds political strength, not parliamentary votes. After the Third Reading of the Trade Union Bill in November 2015, McDonnell marched quickly out into the Central Lobby and across the road to a small demonstration of no more than forty trade unionists, the kind who live and breathe 'the struggle'. He told them that there is too little parliamentarians can do, and too little Labour can do in parliament. It is time to go back to your unions, go back to your communities, and organise. It is time to politicise the strike: threaten that if the government pass the Trade Union Bill, union members will withhold labour.

To elucidate a theory from this idea: industrial action under the remit of the modern state is beholden to capital when it is constrained within the rules and regulations of that state. But there have been times when industrial action has not been about short term withholding of labour in order to gain short term goals – rather, it has been used to interrupt the order of society, to demonstrate the force of organised labour, and to make the ruling classes concede power. This is an ancient tactic. From the 5th century BC when the plebs left Rome in the *Secessio Plebis* (*Secession of the Plebs*) in order to force the patricians to make political decisions in their favour, to the idea of the Grand National Holiday in 1832, a general strike during which workers could take a census so that a new political economy could be devised, socialists have been touting strikes to agitate, gather information about the enemy, and organise for an alternative political economy. Strike them down for a day – and the results will last for a lifetime.

Socialists in Scotland should respond to the impasse of constitutional politics and SNP dominance by finding new terrain. We should abandon the old and stale parliamentary furniture that was crafted, both in Scotland and in Britain, to bear and balance the weight of contending classes. Lacking force to take control, we need the wit and wile to see the hook sticking out of the bait that parliamentary socialism dangles in front of us. This SNP government will be as fickle as the last, Holyrood will bore itself to tears, and a socialist Labour leader holds no golden ticket. Many socialists, with influence in leftward-shifting parties, are digging themselves trenches. They are going to get shelled. We need to go over the top.

Blossom: What Scotland Needs to Flourish

Lesley Riddoch
ISBN 978–1-910021–70-5 PBK £11.99

Since the referendum, bystanders have become organisers, followers have become leaders, politics has become creative, women have become assertive, men have learned to facilitate not dominate. Independent action and self-reliance have helped create a 'can-do' approach shared by almost everyone active in Scotland today. Scotland's biggest problems haven't changed. But we have.

Weeding out vital components of Scottish identity from decades of political and social tangle is no mean task, but it's one journalist Lesley Riddoch has undertaken. Dispensing with the tired, yo-yo-ing jousts over fiscal commissions, Devo Something and EU in-or-out, Blossom pinpoints both the buds of growth and the blight that's holding Scotland back. Drawing from its people and history as well as the experience of the Nordic countries, and the author's own passionate and outspoken perspective, this is a plain-speaking but incisive call to restore equality and control to local communities and let Scotland flourish.

Radical Scotland: Arguments for Self-Determination

Edited by Gerry Hassan and Rosie Illet
ISBN: 978-1-906817-94-7 PBK £12.99

The era of devolution as we have known it is over. Radical Scotland *challenges conventional wisdoms, and poses solutions which encourage us to become more active agents of our own destiny.*

Scotland believes it is a radical, egalitarian, inclusive nation. It was hoped that the establishment of the Scottish Parliament was going to give expression to this. Instead, we have witnessed a minimal, unattractive politics with little to choose between the main parties. This might be adequate in the good times, but no more.

Radical Scotland: Arguments for Self-Determination explores how we can go beyond the limited politics we have experienced and makes the case for shifting from self-government politically to self-determination as a society and a nation. This book is a must read for all those interested in Scotland at a crucial time, for its future, for the Parliament, and for those who want our politics and public policy to be more effective, imaginative and bold.

What Would Keir Hardie Say?
Exploring his vision and relevance to 21st Century politics
Edited by Pauline Bryan
ISBN 978–1-91002115-1 PBK £9.99

My work has consisted of trying to stir up a divine discontent with wrong.—KEIR HARDIE

Has the Labour Party stayed true to Hardie's socialist ideals and vision?

What would Hardie make of the recent developments in Scottish politics?

If he were active today, what would Keir Hardie say about attacks on welfare • trade union rights • immigration • privatisation • European Union • the economy?

Keir Hardie, founder and first leader of the Labour Party, was a stringent critic of the world he saw around him. A socialist, a trade unionist and above all an agitator, he gave unstinting support to the women's suffrage movement and risked all in his commitment to anti-imperialism and international peace.

Marking the centenary of Hardie's death, writers, trade unionists, academics and politicians reflect on Hardie's contribution and what it means today.

Small Nations in a Big World
Michael Keating and Malcolm Harvey
ISBN 978–1-910021–20-0 PBK £9.99

Small nations can do well in the global marketplace, yet they face the world in very different ways. Some accept market logic and take the 'low road' of low wages, low taxes and light regulation, with a correspondingly low level of public services. Others take the 'high road' of social investment, which entails a larger public sector and higher taxes. Such a strategy requires innovative government, flexibility and social partnership. Keating and Harvey compare the experience of the Nordic and Baltic states and Ireland, which have taken very different roads and ask what lessons can be learnt for Scotland. They conclude that Scotland could be made to work as an independent state but this implies not merely a change its external relations or formal status, but a rebuilding of its institutions internally. We know from the example of other small states that this requires bold decisions and hard choices.

Luath Press Limited

committed to publishing well written books worth reading

LUATH PRESS takes its name from Robert Burns, whose little collie Luath (*Gael.*, swift or nimble) tripped up Jean Armour at a wedding and gave him the chance to speak to the woman who was to be his wife and the abiding love of his life. Burns called one of the 'Twa Dogs' Luath after Cuchullin's hunting dog in Ossian's *Fingal*.

Luath Press was established in 1981 in the heart of Burns country, and is now based a few steps up the road from Burns' first lodgings on Edinburgh's Royal Mile. Luath offers you distinctive writing with a hint of unexpected pleasures.

Most bookshops in the UK, the US, Canada, Australia, New Zealand and parts of Europe, either carry our books in stock or can order them for you. To order direct from us, please send a £sterling cheque, postal order, international money order or your credit card details (number, address of cardholder and expiry date) to us at the address below. Please add post and packing as follows: UK – £1.00 per delivery address; overseas surface mail – £2.50 per delivery address; overseas airmail – £3.50 for the first book to each delivery address, plus £1.00 for each additional book by airmail to the same address. If your order is a gift, we will happily enclose your card or message at no extra charge.

Luath Press Limited
543/2 Castlehill
The Royal Mile
Edinburgh EH1 2ND
Scotland
Telephone: +44 (0)131 225 4326 (24 hours)
Email: sales@luath. co.uk
Website: www. luath.co.uk